Date Due

GLOBAL FINANCIAL MARKETS REVOLUTION

GLOBAL
FINANCIAL MARKETS
REVOLUTION

The Future of Exchanges and Global Capital Markets

Hemendra Aran
and
Alpesh B. Patel

First published 2006 by
PALGRAVE MACMILLAN
Houndmills, Basingstoke, Hampshire RG21 6XS and
175 Fifth Avenue, New York, N.Y. 10010
Companies and representatives throughout the world

PALGRAVE MACMILLAN is the global academic imprint of the Palgrave Macmillan division of St. Martin's Press, LLC and of Palgrave Macmillan Ltd. Macmillan® is a registered trademark in the United States, United Kingdom and other countries. Palgrave is a registered trademark in the European Union and other countries.

ISBN-13: 978–1–4039–4621–8
ISBN-10: 1–4039–4621–3

This book is printed on paper suitable for recycling and made from fully managed and sustained forest sources.

A catalogue record for this book is available from the British Library.

A catalog record for this book is available from the Library of Congress.

10   9   8   7   6   5   4   3   2   1
15 14 13 12 11 10 09 08 07 06

Printed and bound in Great Britain by
Creative Print & Design (Wales), Ebbw Vale

Hemendra Aran would like to dedicate the book
to his mother, Mrs Lalita Aran and his
aunt, Mrs Satyabhama Baranwal

Both authors would like to dedicate the book to the
Aranca team who contributed to the book:
Mrs Soma Dhar
Mr Madhusudan Rajagopalan
Mrs Deepti Machavolu

CONTENTS

Contents

CASE STUDIES

The Need for the Book

The recent phenomenal changes in equity, derivatives and commodity exchanges, fuelled by technology and globalization, are opening opportunities for exchanges, investment banks, lawyers, listed companies, and capital markets generally.

For instance, the Chicago Mercantile Exchange became the first publicly traded US financial exchange in December 2002. By 2006 NASDAQ will end its inter-market service, China is making large changes to its services to make it easier for fund managers to use its exchanges, the five ASEAN countries are to create regional FTSE indices, and even Vietnam is seeing a surge of trading on its stock exchange.

Yet the changes are so profound, some question whether we need exchanges at all. The New York Stock Exchange (NYSE) trading floor will see the 213-year-old institution allow unrestricted trading via computers, its biggest customers likely executing most of their transactions without human intervention. Consequently, 3000 floor traders and clerks who now handle about 90 percent of the NYSE's business will be out of a job.

Despite the market capitalization of companies listed on exchanges running into trillions of dollars worldwide, there is no mainstream book using extensive research, to address the major issues facing the whole industry and those who service it.

The contents of this book include:

History and evolution	Historical background
	Nature of capital markets – primary and secondary
	Trading instruments
	Trading systems
	Trading cycle
	Fragmentation, internationalization, liquidity, accessibility, transparency, efficiency
	How we got here
Impact of new technologies	The internet
	Telecommunications
	Technology services
	Best execution
	Where next?
	Gaps and problems for exchanges
	Lessons from some of the most innovative exchanges
The future of exchanges	Who needs stock exchanges?
	Structural trends
	Integration and consolidation
	New products and services
	Efficiencies – who is best?
	Costs
	Clearing and settlement
	Opportunities
Regulation and investor protection	Evolution
	Legal framework
	Regulatory bodies
	Self-regulation
	Regulatory arbitrage
	International cooperation
	Hurdles
	The shape of things to come

Who Should Read This Book?

- Senior management of exchanges – hundreds of exchanges worldwide

- Professional services dealing with exchanges and IPOs, law firms and accountants

- Investment banks

- Consultancies

- Research houses

- Software companies

- Regulators

- Clearing houses

ALPESH B. PATEL
HEMENDRA ARAN

LIST OF ACRONYMS

AMEX	American Stock Exchange	MoU	memorandum of understanding
ATSs	alternative trading systems		
CBOT	Chicago Board of Trade	MTFs	multilateral trading facilities
CCP	central counterparty	NASD	National Association of Securities Dealers
CESR	Committee of European Securities Regulation		
		NSCC	National Securities Clearing Corporation
CME	Chicago Mercantile Exchange		
CSDs	Central Securities Depositories	NYSE	New York Stock Exchange
		PCAOB	Public Company Accounting Oversight Board
DJIA	Dow Jones Industrial Average		
DMA	direct market access	RIE	recognized investment exchange
DPOs	direct public offerings		
DTC	Depository Trust Company	SAI	statement of additional information
DTCC	Depository Trust and Clearing Corporation		
		SBU	strategic business unit
ECNs	electronic communication networks	SEC	Securities Exchange Commission
		SIPC	Securities Investor Protection Corporation
ETFs	exchange-traded funds		
FSA	Financial Services Authority (UK)	SROs	self-regulatory organizations
		SSFs	single stock futures
IC	intermediary custodian	SSSs	securities settlement systems
ICSDs	international central securities depositories	STP	straight through processing
		UC	ultimate custodian
ICT	information and communications technology	UITs	unit investment trusts
		WDM	wholesale debt market
IPO	initial public offering		
LSE	London Stock Exchange		

CHAPTER 1

The History and Evolution of Financial Markets

The first broker …

The evolution of financial markets dates back to twelfth-century France where the *courratier de change* managed and regulated the debts of the agricultural communities on behalf of the banks. The *courratier de change* was thus the first broker in the financial markets.

… to the first "bourse" …

In the late thirteenth century, the commodity traders of Bruges (now Belgium) gathered inside the house of a man called Van der Bourse for trading in commodities. In 1309, they institutionalized these informal meetings and called them the "Bruges Bourse". The idea quickly spread to neighboring counties and such bourses opened in Ghent and Amsterdam. The Bruges Bourse can technically be called the first exchange.

… and the first publicly issued security

The first publicly issued security can be traced back to the fourteenth century in Venice where the government made the first known issue of bonds. These government securities were purchased by merchants and landowners as investments.

The Dutch later started joint stock companies, which permitted shareholders to invest in business ventures and obtain a share in the profits – or losses. In 1602, the Dutch East India Company issued the first shares on the

Amsterdam Stock Exchange. It was the first company to issue stocks and bonds.

By the eighteenth century, the first stock exchanges were formed in England, the Netherlands and France. In the American colonies, commerce was significant, but still heavily controlled by England.

Around the 1750s in England, traders in the shares of early companies would meet in Jonathan's Coffee House to trade shares and make business deals. Early share bids and offers were written on the Coffee House walls and the trading process was highly unregulated, with insider trading forming the basis for most investment decisions. By 1773, trading clubs had formed, and in 1801 a group of traders raised £20,000 to build the London Stock Exchange (LSE) in Capel Court.

A similar process occurred in America. By the early 1790s many brokers had begun trading in shares. These brokers too would meet informally in coffee houses. In 1792, 24 such brokers signed the Buttonwood Tree Agreement and paid $400 for a "trading seat". The Buttonwood Tree Agreement formed the basis for trading rules that still exist today and led to the formation in 1817 of the New York Stock Exchange.

Over the years, stock exchanges have opened up across the globe and most important financial centers have at least one exchange. Modern stock exchanges have grown to have an unprecedented number of listed stocks as well as stockbrokers.

What is a Stock Exchange?

A stock exchange is often the most important component of a stock market. A stock exchange is a centralized and organized market for the trading of stocks and bonds. By providing a centralized market for the exchange of securities, stock exchanges greatly facilitate the financing of business through the flotation of stocks and bonds. Such markets were originally open to all, but over the years only members of a particular exchange can trade on that exchange. A stock can be traded on an exchange only if it is listed on that particular exchange. For a particular stock to be listed on an exchange, the stock should fulfil certain listing criteria. Apart from certain common listing requirements, specific listing requirements vary from exchange to exchange.

Evolution from "location" ...

Historically, exchanges have evolved from a "location" where buyers and sellers of securities congregated for transacting business. Slowly the exchange took on the function of settling disputes that arose during the course of the transactions. This led to the exchange formulating certain "regulations" to protect the innocents from the professionals, thereby making it attractive to the public to keep using the exchange for trading. To attract financially sound companies to the exchange, it began to develop "listing regulations". These listing regulations stipulated the minimum requirements a company must satisfy to enlist on that exchange. With the development of the stock ticker, exchanges were able to disseminate last sale information – "market data" – that served as advertisements for the market and provided transparency that made prospective investors comfortable with the fairness of the market. As the volume of transactions increased,

... to a congregation satisfying various needs of its members

the exchanges had to provide for "clearing and settlement" functions. The exchanges themselves began performing these functions or provided an agency to perform these two operations.

Stock exchanges provided these services at minimal cost to their members as their existence was mainly to serve their members at the lowest cost possible. Historically, exchanges had the following main sources of revenue:

■ Membership fees

■ Listing fees

■ Trading fees

■ Clearing and settlement fees

■ Fees from the provision of market data.

The stock market comprises two markets – the primary market and the secondary market.

Primary market

The primary market is the market for the initial issuance of securities. The primary market does not require a stock exchange. An organization that requires funds contacts its investment banker who typically assembles a syndicate of securities dealers who will sell the new stock issue. These securities that are sold to prospective investors are called initial public offerings (IPOs). An IPO is the company's first sale of common shares to the investing public.

Secondary market

Once the company makes its first sale of common shares to the public, it has to ensure liquidity for the investing public. To ensure liquidity, the company has to enlist itself on one or more exchanges. Enlistment on a stock exchange ensures a secondary market for the company. In the secondary market, investors purchase securities from other investors rather than the issuers, subsequent to the original issuance in the primary market.

Trading Instruments

Typically a stock exchange permits its member brokers to deal in equities (shares issued by companies), gilts (bonds issued by the government) and derivatives.

Equities

When an investor buys shares in a company, the investor becomes a partial owner of that company. The principal benefit to the shareholder is to receive a share of the profits – usually in the form of dividends. Apart from regular dividend payments, a rise in the profitability or prospects of mergers or acquisitions drive the share prices upwards. Likewise, the prospect of falling profits depresses the market price of the particular equity. Since companies issue a fixed number of shares, the market-driven forces of supply and demand increase or depress the share price of a stock. Investors with a high risk appetite should invest in equities.

Gilts

Gilts are sold by the government to the investing public to fund the shortfall in its expenditure over its tax collection. The investor in this case earns a fixed rate of return on a predetermined redemption date. Normally, the interest on a gilt is fixed throughout its life, no matter how low general interest rates fall. The price of gilts can however rise or fall in the market depending on the outlook for interest rates and inflation changes, providing possible opportunities to sell at a profit before redemption. For risk-averse investors, gilts offer a good opportunity for investments.

Derivatives

In the past two decades, derivatives have become increasingly important as a trading instrument. Futures and options are actively traded throughout the world. Forward contracts, swaps and many different types of options are regularly traded outside exchanges by financial institutions, fund managers and corporate treasurers in the "over-the-counter" market. Derivatives are also sometimes added to a bond or stock issue.

A derivative can be defined as a financial instrument whose value depends on (or derives from) the values of other more basic underlying variables. Very often the variables underlying derivatives are the prices of traded assets. For example, a stock option is a derivative whose value is dependent on the price of the stock. However, derivatives can be dependent on almost any variable, from the price of cotton to the amount of rainfall expected.

Exchange Traded Markets

Futures contract

A derivatives exchange is a market where investors trade standardized contracts that have been defined by the exchange. Derivatives exchanges have existed for a long time. The Chicago Board of Trade (CBOT) was established in 1848 to bring farmers and merchants together. Initially its main task was to standardize the quantities and qualities of the grains that were traded. Within a few years, the first futures-type contract was developed, known as a "to-arrive" contract. Speculators preferred to trade in this type of contract as it was an attractive alternative to trading the grain itself. In 1919, the Chicago Mercantile Exchange (CME) was established. Currently, futures exchanges exist in all parts of the world.

Options contract

The Chicago Board Options Exchange (CBOE) started trading call options contracts on 16 stocks in 1973. Options had traded prior to 1973, but the CBOE was successful in creating an orderly market with well-defined contracts. Put option contracts started trading on the exchange in 1977. The CBOE now trades options on over 1200 stocks and many different stock indices. Like futures, options contracts have also been very popular and are traded globally. The underlying assets include foreign currencies and futures contracts as well as stocks and stock indices.

Traditionally, derivatives traders used the open outcry system for trading in derivative products. However, in recent years, exchanges have increasingly moved from the open outcry system to electronic trading. Eventually, as exchanges change to electronic trading systems, derivatives trading will also shift to electronic platforms.

Over-the-counter Markets

As in stock trading, derivatives trading is done outside the exchange using the telecommunication network. Traders do not meet physically but use the telephone and the computer network via the internet for trading in derivatives. The over-the-counter market is normally restricted to institutional investors and corporate clients. Financial institutions often act as market makers for the commonly traded instruments. This means that they are always prepared to quote both a bid price (a price at which they are prepared to buy) and an offer price (a price at which they are prepared to sell).

Telephone conversations in the over-the-counter market are usually taped. If there is a dispute about what was agreed, the tapes are replayed to resolve the issue. Trades in the over-the-counter market are typically larger than trades in the exchange traded market. A key advantage of the over-the-counter market is that the terms of the contract do not have to be those specified by an exchange. Market participants are free to negotiate any mutually attractive deal. A disadvantage is that there is usually some credit risk in an over-the-counter trade (that is, there is a small risk that the contract will not be honored).

Forward Contracts

A forward contract is a particularly simple derivative. It is an agreement to buy or sell an asset at a specified future time for a certain price. It can be contrasted with a "spot contract", which is an agreement to buy or sell an asset today. A forward contract is traded on the over-the-counter market – usually between two financial institutions or between a financial institution and one of its clients.

One of the parties to a forward contract assumes a long position and agrees to buy the underlying asset on a specified future date for a specified price. The other party assumes a short position and agrees to sell the asset on the same date for the same price.

Forward contracts on foreign exchanges are very popular. Most large banks have a "forward desk" within their foreign exchange trading room that is devoted to the trading of forward contracts. Forward contracts can be used to hedge foreign currency risk.

Forward price and
delivery price

It is important to distinguish between the forward price and the delivery price. The forward price is the market price that would be agreed to today for delivery of the asset on a specified maturity date. The forward price is usually different from the spot price and varies with the maturity date.

Futures Contracts

Like a forward contract, a futures contract is an agreement between two parties to buy or sell an asset at a certain time in the future for a certain price. Unlike forward contracts, futures contracts are normally traded on an exchange. To make trading possible, the exchange specifies certain standardized features of the contract. As the two parties to the contract do not necessarily know each other, the exchange also provides a mechanism that gives the two parties a guarantee that the contract will be honored.

The largest exchanges on which futures contracts are traded are the CBOT and the CME. On these and other exchanges worldwide, a wide range of commodities and financial assets form the underlying assets in the various contracts. The commodities include pork bellies, live cattle, sugar, wool, lumber, copper, aluminum, gold and tin. The financial assets include stock indices, currencies and Treasury bonds.

The only difference between a futures contract and a forward contract is that an exact delivery date is not specified. The contract is referred to by its delivery month and the exchange specifies the period during the month when delivery must be made. For commodities, the delivery period is usually the entire month. The holder of the short position has the right to choose the time during the delivery period when it will make delivery. Usually, contracts with several different delivery months are traded at any one time. The exchange specifies the amount of asset to be delivered for one contract and how the futures price is to be quoted. In the case of a commodity, the exchange also specifies the product quality and the delivery location.

Options

Options are traded on exchanges and in the over-the-counter market. There are two basic types of options. A "call option" gives the holder the right to buy the underlying asset by a certain date for a certain price. A "put option" gives the holder the right to sell the underlying asset by a certain date for a certain price. The price in the contract is known as the "exercise price" or strike price; the date in the contract is known as the "expiration date" or maturity. *American options* can be exercised at any time up to the expiration date. *European options* can be exercised only on the expiration date itself. In the exchange traded equity options market, one contract is usually an agreement to buy or sell 100 shares. European options are generally easier to analyze than American options and some of the properties of an American option are frequently deduced from those of its European counterpart.

American and European-style options

There is a significant difference between an options contract and a futures contract. In an options contract, the holder of the contract has the right to exercise the contract. But he need not exercise that right. In a futures contract, the holder has to exercise the underlying contract – that is, he is obligated to buy or sell the underlying asset. Another difference between an options and a futures contract is that whereas it costs nothing to enter into a forward or futures contract, there is a cost for acquiring an options contract.

Other Derivatives

There is virtually no limit to the innovations that are possible in the derivatives area. Some of the options traded in the over-the-counter markets have payoffs dependent on the maximum value attained by a variable during a period of time; some have payoffs dependent on the average value of a variable during a period of time; some have exercise prices that are functions of time; some have features where exercising one option automatically gives the holder another option; some have payoffs dependent on the square of a future interest rate and so on.

Traditionally, the variables underlying options and other derivatives have been stock prices, stock indices, interest rates, exchange rates and commodity prices. However, other underlying variables are becoming increasingly common. For example, the payoffs from credit derivatives depend on the creditworthiness of one or more companies; weather derivatives have payoffs dependent on the average temperature at particular locations; insurance derivatives have payoffs dependent on the dollar amount of insurance claims of a specified type made during a specified period; and electricity derivatives have payoffs dependent on the spot price of electricity.

Types of Derivatives Traders

There are broadly three types of derivatives traders. They are hedgers, speculators and arbitrageurs. Hedgers use futures, forwards and options to reduce the risk that they face from potential future movements in a market variable. Speculators use them to bet on the future direction of a market variable. Arbitrageurs take offsetting positions in two or more instruments to lock in a profit.

Trading Systems

Congregation of buyers
and sellers openly
shouting out their orders

Open outcry – Traditionally stock exchanges have been a centralized location where buyers and sellers meet physically and, depending on the demand and supply of a particular equity, prices are set. This is the "open outcry" system where the prices of the different stocks are set by openly calling out aloud. The centralized location is usually the "trading floor" or "trading pit". "Specialists" are physically present on the exchanges' trading floors. Here each specialist specializes in a particular stock, buying and selling in a verbal auction.

Buyers and sellers
connected by a
telecommunication
network

Electronic exchanges – The traditional open outcry system is slowly giving way to electronic exchanges. These electronic exchanges eliminate the need for specialist traders, while drastically reducing the execution time of a trade and thus lowering the cost of trading. Electronic trading systems are screen-based and buyers and sellers need not be physically present on the trading floor. Buyers and sellers are connected by computers over a telecommunications network. Market makers, also known as "dealers", carry their own inventory of stocks and are required to post their bid and ask prices on the network.

Trading takes place in
a ubiquitous computer
network ...

Alternative trading systems (ATSs) – These have evolved in recent times. Trading takes place in a ubiquitous computer network. ATSs trade listed stocks, but they connect buyers and sellers directly. ATSs usually deal in bulk orders and therefore are used increasingly by institutional investors. Since the ATSs are in direct competition with stock exchanges, trading costs are substantially lower. Moreover, they provide real-time execution as well as access to equity markets worldwide and innovative investment categories. However, ATSs do not service retail investors. Both stock exchanges and ATSs bring securities buyers and sell-

... and is not governed by any market supervisory authorities

ers together. The key distinction between them is that transactions via the ATSs are based on private law contracts, not on stock exchange law. In addition, stock exchanges have to meet stricter regulatory requirements. Off-exchange markets have neither admission procedures for securities nor a market supervisory authority.

Cross-border trading and extended trading hours widen scope for investors to trade on ATSs

ATSs offer investors wider trading opportunities by providing extended trading hours, access to equity markets worldwide and innovative investment types such as financial instruments from the private equity segment. Moreover, ATSs facilitate after-hours trading and well-informed traders can benefit immensely. ATSs draw on the advantages their specialization gives them over conventional stock exchanges in order to provide investors with customized market models. However, the ATSs do not offer clearing and settlement functions. This function is the exclusive domain of the stock exchanges. With ATSs offering lower trading costs, most stock exchanges will be compelled to lower their trading costs. However, since the stock exchanges cover the entire value chain of business from trading to clearing and settlement, they will have to cover their costs out of revenues from clearing and settlement.

Clearing and Settlement

The penultimate stage of the secondary market operation

Historically, stock exchanges have performed the function of clearing and settlement of transactions that have taken place on the exchange. The buying or selling of equities is only the initial function in a transaction. For the transaction to be fully executed, the exchange has to perform the clearing and settlement functions too. The first stage of the clearing and settlement function is that the actual deliveries of the shares concerned have to be taken from the seller, whilst the buyer of the shares has to make payment for the shares purchased. In the second stage, the seller will receive the payment due whilst the buyer takes physical delivery of the shares.

With regulators in most countries enforcing quicker clearing and settlement norms, trading cycles in most exchanges are shortening. Moreover, with most exchanges shifting to electronic trading systems, it is becoming increasingly possible for exchanges to have shorter trading cycles. Currently, most exchanges across Europe, America and the Asia-Pacific region follow a T+3 trading cycle and many of them are trying to reduce the trading cycle to T+1.

What is the T+3 Trading System?

The T+3 trading system means that when you buy shares, your payment must be received by your brokerage firm no later than three business days after the trade is executed. And if you sell securities, your brokerage firm must receive your share certificate no later than three business days after you authorized the sale.

What is the Best Trading System?

At the outset it is difficult to conclude which is the best trading system. While open outcry had the advantage of setting a market price according to supply and demand, electronic trading systems eliminate the need for a market maker, thereby reducing the cost of trading. With information freely available, investors will choose the trading system they feel is best. Investors prefer to use the exchange or trading system where they believe their orders have the greatest chance of being executed. Exchanges and trading systems in turn try to offer various incentives to attract customers by offering a low price, including transaction, clearing and listing services. To attract more customers to their trading system, exchanges compete among themselves. This may lead to fragmentation of business as investors may choose to trade on a number of trading venues instead of a single trading venue. This fragmentation of trading reduces the liquidity in each of the trading venues, thereby increasing the volatility of transaction prices.

Competition among trading systems leads to fragmentation of business …

However, market structures are constantly evolving, and activities move in response to innovations in trading and the development of financial instruments. In the long run, unfettered competitive pressures will foster consolidation, as liquidity tends to centralize in the system providing the narrowest bid–ask spreads at volume. Two or more venues trading the same security or commodity will naturally converge towards a single market. One market offering marginally narrower bid–ask spreads at volume will attract the business of others, further improving its liquidity and reducing that of its competitors. This in turn will create an even greater competitive imbalance, eventually leading to full consolidation. Of course, this process may not be fully realized if there are impediments to competition or if markets are able to establish and secure niches by competing on factors other than price.

… but later fosters consolidation and consequently improves liquidity

Under the electronic trading systems, not all trades are reported in the market due to internalization (a process whereby certain transactions may be internally crossed off) by the intermediaries and consequently the investor does not get the best possible deal. Secondly, internal-

Internalization

ization diverts "uninformed", low risk trades away from the primary exchange, leaving only the more "informed" and higher risk orders on the primary exchange. This may lead dealers to set wider spreads on the primary exchange in order to protect themselves from being picked off by investors with better information. However, internalization also benefits investors if they choose to trade on the ATSs, since ATSs compete directly with the primary exchange, leading to investors getting a better deal by way of a better price as well as lower dealing costs than on the primary exchange.

Fragmentation and internalization together drive down transaction costs

Considering the above two trends of fragmentation and internalization, exchanges will be compelled to drive down their transaction costs as well as ensure liquidity. To recapture their market share which has been moving towards the ATSs, many exchanges worldwide have cut trading costs. But for the exchanges' existence, liquidity is more important and sustaining value from customers through value-added services and market practices and brand-building activities are the key factors. To ensure liquidity, exchanges have to provide better connectivity to their customers at lower costs, and also make membership procedures simpler.

Technological advancement ensures cross-border trades and consequently enhances liquidity

Better connectivity will ensure cross-border trades, and the exchanges' revenue stream could be expanded across borders if exchanges can ensure better liquidity. However, the ATSs may be a better option for cross-border trades since most ATSs trade across several exchanges across countries. Primary exchanges will have to make significant improvements like providing single screens for multiproduct cross-border trading to retain and add to their customer base. Bigger exchanges have set up trading hubs across nations to facilitate cross-border trading activities and also offer after-hours trading options.

A fully transparent market ensures best execution

The level of transparency in a market ensures the level of competition between the trading systems. Greater transparency improves informational efficiency, thereby facilitating arbitrage between different systems, thus ensuring price priority and enhancing the price discovery process. This in turn enhances best execution.

However, sometimes bigger investors may not be willing to expose their orders publicly and would prefer to use ATSs. This would decrease the liquidity in the system. Transparency is however a double-edged sword, whereby under certain circumstances it may help to stabilize speculation and absorb order flow imbalances and reduce volatility. At other times, it may exacerbate market participants' strategic behavior towards each other, with the possibility of increasing volatility.

CHAPTER 2

The Impact of New Technologies

Technology enabled the shift from open outcry to screen-based trading

Technology has revolutionized the operations of stock exchanges. With the advent of computers, securities transactions that were once slow and dependent on expensive human labor have become instantaneous and inexpensive. Since the 1990s, most exchanges the world over have moved to screen-based trading systems. The earlier floor-based trading systems precluded the possibility of linkage with other exchanges due to limitations of space. The development of screen-based systems has enabled linkages to be established between the exchanges. Trading via the internet was instantly accepted and most retail investors with a computer and an internet connection preferred to trade from the luxury of their homes. Newer exchanges have adopted the fully electronic trading systems which have lowered the costs of setting up and consequently these exchanges can charge lower fees to their members.

Technology increases trading volumes …

Improvements in technology and the advent of electronic trading have increased the speed of transactions, while providing wider access to stock markets. The alternative trading systems allow round the clock trading. These key factors – speed and access – have resulted in an explosion of trading volumes.

… helps to provide information …

Information is central to the investment advisory industry. New computer and electronic communica-

… in a fraction of a second …

tion systems have made enormous amounts of financial information more readily available to both investment advisers and investors. New technologies allow advisers to gather, assimilate and analyze information faster and less expensively than ever before. This information has allowed many individual investors to learn more about their investments, and about the type of questions that they should ask when dealing with investment advisers.

… and helps investment advisers to provide better services to their clients

Technology in turn has helped investment advisers to gather more information and thereby provide enhanced services to their clients. Advisers must choose those investments that are suitable for their clients. Investment research and the ability to analyze vast amounts of information are the key elements of a typical adviser's decision-making process. The large amount of information currently available due to technological developments permits advisers to learn about opportunities that they would not otherwise know about and has helped them to serve their clients better.

Technology aids clearing

"Clearing" has been defined by the Committee on Payment and Settlement Systems (CPSS) as "the process of transmitting, reconciling and in some cases, confirming payment orders or security transfer instructions prior to settlement". In recent years, many leading stock exchanges like the LSE and the Euronext have introduced central counterparty (CCP) clearing for share trading using clearing houses such as Crestco and Euroclear. CCP essentially involves splitting every trade into two – one between the seller and the CCP (the buyer) and other between the buyer and the CCP (the seller). In effect, the CCP becomes the buyer to every seller and the seller to every buyer. CCP clearing has a number of advantages as it eliminates counterparty risk and systematic risk, and provides anonymity, netting and cost reduction.

Technology aids settlement Settlement represents the payment and delivery of stocks. Whenever funds are not transferred automatically through cash accounts at the central securities depositories (CSDs), other central banks are often used. The relationship between settlement and payment is becoming increasingly seamless with the promotion of straight through processing (STP). This is a communications process that transfers information electronically to all parties involved in the trade simultaneously rather than sequentially. STP therefore provides a way to reduce trading failures (as the same information is sent out to all parties) and reduces costs (data does not have to be manually entered again and again).

The Internet

Internet aids faster and deeper reach to clients … In the last couple of years, markets and market professionals have adopted internet technology widely to enhance their communication networks. Securities firms have begun using internet technologies for intranets. With intranets, firms can create information repositories that are easily accessible by all within the firm. This information can also be provided to institutional clients through extranets.

… by providing a vast array of information to actual and potential clients Broker-dealer websites perform a variety of functions. Firstly, they advertise the broker-dealers' services to potential investors. Secondly, they may also offer market information and investment tools similar to those offered by information vendors. Some broker-dealers' websites offer real-time or delayed quote information and allow investors to create a personal stock ticker. Some also provide market summaries and commentaries, analyst reports and trading strategies, and market data on currencies, mutual funds, options, market indices and news. In addition, there are also a number of broker-dealers who offer investors access to portfolio management tools and analytic programs. A typical site will include information on commission fees, branch office locations and places where the broker-dealer is qualified to trade. Full service brokers emphasize the availability of account information and research reports and, in some cases, provide their registered representatives with their own home pages. A small number of broker-dealers, usually discount brokers, allow investors to access their account information and enter orders to purchase or sell securities on the internet.

Internet stock dealing has been quite well accepted

Online stock trading via the internet has been quite well publicized and has also been well accepted by retail investors. Online stock trading via the internet offers investors the flexibility of trading from their homes. Most broker-dealers require their customers to use an internet browser that supports encryption, considering this level of encryption to be sufficient to protect their information flows. Typically, a broker-dealer offering internet trading facilities to his/her customers provides an electronic template for the customer to enter the name of the security, the type of transaction – that is, whether the security has to be bought or sold – the quantity of shares to be bought or sold and whether the order is to be executed at the market rate or at a limit price set by the customer. Once the broker-dealer receives this information from his/her customer, it is checked electronically against the customer's account. If the customer has any discrepancies, such as the customer has a "sell" order for a security that he/she does not own or if a "buy" order is given by the customer but he/she lacks the funds to "buy", the order will not be executed. If the customer has no such discrepancies, the order will be routed out of the broker-dealer system immediately and will be executed in a few seconds in the appropriate exchange or market maker. After the order is executed, the customer receives a message confirming the order. If the broker-dealer has a sophisticated system, then the customer's portfolio will also be updated online to reflect the transaction.

A vast array of financial information is available currently online for internet users. With investors becoming more computer savvy, more investment advisers have begun to provide advisory services online. Advisers also have begun to advertise their services using their own websites or sites with information about a number of investment advisers. Developments in computer technologies also enable advisers to offer new types of advisory services to clients.

Advisory services by investment advisers via the internet are picking up fast

Future trends in technology will continue to change the relationship between investment advisers and their clients. As advisers and investors learn more about the potential of new technologies, the type of services provided by advisers and the services requested by their clients will continue to develop.

Public companies are also using the internet extensively to communicate with current and potential stockholders

Besides investment advisers, most public companies are also becoming technology savvy. Many public companies have realized that internet technology offers a valuable forum to communicate with their current and potential stockholders. Most public companies have their own websites where they post important developments, like quarterly, half-yearly and annual results, press releases and periodic reports. Such online postings reduce the company's printing and mailing costs. Investors have the ability to search more easily within a document, hyperlink to recent non-financial news and learn about complex matters through the use of hyperlinks to educational material. Most public companies have realized that information is vital for protecting investors. They have realized that an investor can make an informed decision on whether to buy, sell or hold securities, or how to vote on corporate matters, if the investor has full and accurate information about the company and its financial position. However, so far the internet has not fully replaced the traditional paper documentation and this continues to be used when information has to be delivered to specific investors.

The use of internet technologies facilitates the corporate sector in the following manner:

- Information transmission is much faster and more widespread.

- Helps to create a level playing field for small and big companies.

- Helps companies to raise capital more effectively by giving them better access to potential investors.

- Creates an avenue for communication with stockholders.

The internet also enhances the ability of investors and their advisers to make informed decisions in the following manner:

- Faster transmission of information.

- Easier search mechanisms and consequently faster analysis of financial information.

- Reduces disparity between big and small companies.

- Helps investors to communicate with each other and with companies.

The advantages of internet trading are as follows:

- Securities trading has become transparent.

- Significant cost reduction.
- Investors have access to quality stock analysis.

Telecommunications

Technological development removes cross-border barriers and aids the creation of a global equity trading market

Traditionally, stock exchanges emerged in areas of industrial development and have remained localized since then. Newer exchanges also emerged but trading continued to remain localized. Localized literally meant the same city or region. Most industrial regions the world over had at least one or more stock exchanges. The listing of shares also remained localized according to proximity. Multiple listings were also confined within the country. Cross-border listings were completely unheard of. Most companies had little choice but to list in the local market; investors, especially retail investors, would invest mainly in the local market, which was accessed through locally based intermediaries. Technological improvements have changed this scenario dramatically.

Technology has removed the geographical barriers for the cross-border trading of equity shares. Until recently, if a local investor was interested in buying or selling a particular stock listed in a foreign country, he/she had to contact his/her local broker-dealer. This local broker-dealer would in turn get in touch with a broker-dealer of the foreign stock exchange where the stock was listed and convey the order. After the order was executed by the foreign broker-dealer in the listed country's exchange, he/she would convey the deal back to the originating broker-dealer who in turn would convey it to his/her local investor. This was a long drawn out process. However, now it is possible for an investor to obtain real-time information about trading on foreign markets from a number of different sources and directly enter orders electronically from his/her home country. Many exchanges the world over are shifting to electronic trading systems to attract foreign equity trading. Investors from anywhere in the world can buy or sell in any other country without being physically present "on" that exchange. Several foreign markets have begun offering remote access by establishing trading hubs.

Technology is vital for the development of capital markets

Information and communications technology (ICT) is critical to the development of healthy and efficient capital markets – both primary and secondary. The markets have been quick to assimilate any new technological advances that the capital market has witnessed. These new developments have increased market efficiencies and enhanced the flow of information into capital markets. In the past decade, tools such as PCs, desktop work stations, networking capabilities, more powerful computer processing and increasingly sophisticated hardware and software have been developed and made commercially available. These recent advances in ICT result in more efficient and transparent markets which are better able to handle increased trading volumes. In this respect, the impact of new technologies on the securities industry as a whole has been pervasive. These developments in the telecommunications sector have not been limited to the markets but have extended to the securities industry professionals as well.

Automation of trading systems drastically cuts the time lag for execution and completion of order on stock exchanges

Stock exchanges have automated most of their operations to improve their efficiency. Earlier, processing a securities trade on the exchange floor was a manual, labor-intensive process. Generally, an order received by a broker-dealer's registered representative at a branch office would be telephoned to the firm's order desk, the firm's order desk would telephone the firm's trading booth on the exchange floor and a representative of the broking firm (the floor broker) would take the order to the specialist trader for the particular stock and execute the trade with either the specialist trader or any other trader who may be interested in the stock. If, however, the order was not executable immediately, it was given to the specialist trader and handwritten into the specialist trader's book for future execution. The process of reporting the transaction back to the client was substantially the same in reverse. This system involved a lot of paper work and consequently back office work was considerable. This prompted stock exchanges to develop computerized systems for order delivery and execution. Slowly, further increases in trading volumes also prompted the automation of other functions, such as the dissemination of transaction and quotation information, specialist traders' limit order books and the comparison of trades prior to settlement.

Screen-based trading systems by broker-dealers have eliminated the trading pit

Increasing volumes have also prompted broker-dealers to automate many of their operations. With the development of electronic trading systems, most registered broker-dealers provide an automated, screen-based network through which participants can enter orders or execute trades against orders entered by others. Like the traditional exchanges, these systems centralize orders and give participants control over the interaction of their orders. Information vendors now also provide many of the services historically provided by exchanges or broker-dealers. Many information vendors now offer electronic order routing services as well as financial product data. In addition, some vendors offer trading systems that connect market intermediaries with their clients. These systems are sponsored by particular broker-dealers and are available only to that intermediary's customers. Generally, they enable customers to view the intermediary's inventory, electronically route orders to the intermediary for execution, and receive confirmation of the trade by the vendor's network. In addition, information vendors offer services that route orders between market participants and send clearance and settlement information to clearing corporations.

Technological advances have boosted cross-border listings and aided global trading

Technological advances have also helped the bigger exchanges like the LSE and the NASDAQ to compete to increase their international listings. Moreover, companies also strive hard to gain overseas listings and raise money from overseas issues. Now, with better accessibility, the number of new listings of foreign companies on the LSE and the NASDAQ has risen dramatically. Although these exchanges have formulated stringent norms for enlistment and the trading rules locally are the same for local companies as well as foreign companies listed on the exchanges, there are no cross-border regulations. So far regulations are still jurisdiction-specific; global regulators and global rules have not yet emerged. Although in the short and medium term, a global marketplace cannot be visualized, in the long run it cannot be ruled out.

Communication developments have made the transmission of real-time information cheap

New communications and computer technology have revolutionalized the way information about price and quotes is disseminated. Traditionally, this was a major source of revenue for stock exchanges and also information on the price of stocks was not so freely available. Now with the setting up of electronic trading systems, most broker-dealers transmit the prices to their registered clients freely over the internet and usually with value added. This has led to the creation of a more open flow of information and a loss of the relevance of contractual obligations that prohibit the redistribution of data. Stock exchanges worldwide have consequently lost a part of their revenue. They have preferred to seek some form of commercial gain by requesting that relevant participants pay for the redistribution of data. This has led to revenue growth from this source but at lower rates. However, it has proved beneficial for investors since they have access to real-time information cheaply.

Alternative Trading Systems (ATSs) or Electronic Communication Networks (ECNs)

New trading systems – ATSs /ECNs – an alternative to stock exchanges

Advances in ICT have altered securities trading globally. New trading systems such as ATSs or electronic communication networks (ECNs) have emerged. The ATSs or ECNs are different from stock exchange electronic trading platforms. While the stock exchange electronic trading platform conforms to the regulations set by the relevant stock exchange, the ATSs or ECNs are based on private law contracts. Moreover, only stocks listed on a particular exchange can be traded on the trading platform of that exchange. But the ATSs or ECNs do not have any listing requirements. Moreover, only registered broker-dealers are permitted to trade on the electronic trading platform while any investor can trade on the ATSs or ECNs. While in an exchange trading system, securities orders are merely shown in the electronic order book, under the ATSs or ECNs, trades are automatically executed.

An ATS is a networked application that electronically connects potential buyers and sellers of securities, matching their trades on a predefined criterion. ATSs include call markets, matching systems and crossing networks. In the most basic form, an ATS is an electronic market that links brokers and market makers (who trade on behalf of institutional and retail investors) without having to send the trade through an exchange for execution.

Significantly low trading costs	The trading costs under ATSs or ECNs are significantly lower since the system eliminates the broker-dealer intermediaries. Also, since the ATSs are in direct competition with the exchanges, they have to lower their charges. Moreover, internal competition among the numerous ATSs or ECNs leads to still lower costs being charged.
Longer trading hours	The ATSs or ECNs trade continuously. These systems do not have any trading timings. They operate before and after the traditional trading hours of the stock exchanges. This gives investors access to trade almost 24 hours a day, 365 days a year.
Wider access	While it is impossible for local broker-dealers to be members of various stock exchanges globally, ATSs or ECNs have access to all the global markets. This makes it convenient for investors to trade globally from one base.
Customized services	The ATSs or ECNs can adapt the trading mechanisms according to the requirements of investors and consequently they are able to provide customized services to investors. An investor can choose the method of price discovery and thereafter execute the order. The investor can choose between the crossing system, the quote-driven system, a hit and take system or a call auction system for execution of his or her order. To let investors adapt the degree of transparency to individual transactions, ATSs/ECNs offer both open and anonymous limit order books.
Boosts automation of stock exchanges	The ATSs and ECNs are fully automated and transparent systems and consequently many institutional investors preferred to trade on them. With stock exchanges losing substantial revenue to the ATSs/ECNs, they were compelled to invest huge sums of

money to upgrade their trading systems. Currently, most stock exchanges worldwide have upgraded to electronic trading and clearing systems.

Challenges Faced

Liquidity

The main problem facing ATSs or ECNs is retaining and increasing volumes to increase liquidity. If the ATSs or ECNs are unable to attract volumes, lower prices cannot be maintained and the business model falls apart. Moreover, while trying to meet the regulatory norms set by the stock exchange regulatory boards, most of the ATSs or ECNs have to incur substantial expenditure on technology.

ECNs in the USA

ECNs have been in existence in the US for over three decades. The first ECN to be established was Instinet in 1969. However, since 1996, when the Securities Exchange Commission (SEC) order handling rules compelled stock markets to display their best prices, ECNs have proliferated. Since 1996, ECNs such as Archipelago, Brut, Island, Instinet, and so on have witnessed increasing business from investors. The advantages of trading through these trading systems have made them attractive to investors and consequently the ECNs have been able to take away significant volumes from traditional stock exchanges.

So as not to be totally left behind, the traditional exchanges have responded by shifting to electronic trading systems. However, the ECNs for their part are trying to win back the volumes by consolidating among themselves. SunGuard acquired Brut, Archipelago acquired its rival RediBook and Instinet and Island merged. These mergers have created bigger ECNs which will continue to threaten traditional stock exchanges. The bigger and stronger ECNs have also been installing capital for further technological developments.

In the USA currently, traditional stock exchanges as well as the ECNs are introducing newer pricing schemes to draw customers from each other's region.

ECNs in Europe

In Europe the stock exchanges themselves developed the central order book concept. This has prevented ECNs from making much headway. Volumes for most of these ECNs have been poor and they have mostly been servicing retail clients.

Are ECNs a Threat to Traditional Stock Exchanges?

While ECNs have entered the bastion of the traditional stock exchanges in USA, they have not been able to make much headway in Europe. In the USA, with the consolidation and merger of many ECNs, they have emerged in a stronger position. These ECNs have been able to capture almost 30 percent of the trading volumes from traditional stock exchanges. Unless traditional stock exchanges improve their trading systems, ECNs may emerge stronger than traditional stock exchanges.

Technology Services

Improves disclosures

Technological advances have significantly improved the disclosure techniques of public companies to their current and potential shareholders. Perhaps the most significant technological development relating to public company disclosures is the online availability of the mandated electronic filing database EDGAR in the USA. It is mandatory in the USA for companies to file their earnings (quarterly, half-yearly and annually) and other disclosures regarding the company on the EDGAR. Investors and advisers have free access to this database. Online access to this information reduces a company's printing and mailing costs. Investors have the ability to search more easily within a document, hyperlink to recent non-financial news and learn about complex matters through the use of hyperlinks to educational material.

Electronic media used for raising capital in primary ...

Many issuers and underwriters are using the internet for filing their prospectuses for public offerings. So far a few companies have posted prospectuses on their websites for raising capital directly. These issuers raise capital online through two types of public offers – internet direct public offerings (DPOs) and direct stock purchase plans. A DPO is an offering made without a professional underwriter. DPOs typically are made by small businesses in limited offerings. Using the electronic media does away with the printing and postage costs for small businesses and thereby reduces the cost of raising capital. Although so far DPOs are limited, in the long run this mode of raising capital by small and medium-sized companies is expected to pick up.

... as well as secondary issues

Another area where technological advances have benefited public companies in raising capital is the online foray into direct offerings through their direct stock purchase plans. Direct stock purchase plans provide a vehicle for investors to purchase stock on a periodic basis. Here again the companies save on printing and postage costs.

Annual reports posted on the website

With the electronic media gaining wider coverage, companies have also become more innovative. Many companies have begun to post their annual reports on their website. These annual reports are quite attractive and interactive. Most website annual reports contain information not included in the paper version of the report. Many recent annual reports have included video presentations by senior management, and interactive applications to enable investor feedback. Some annual reports also provide spreadsheets that permit the viewer to analyze the company's financial data.

Electronic or telephone voting

The other area where the electronic media is gaining popularity is electronic voting. Many institutional investors are using internet or telephone voting systems. Many companies also provide electronic access to shareholder meetings. Shareholders from any part of the world can have access to these shareholder meetings. This consolidates the market further and is moving in the direction of creating one global market. Moreover, participants in several proxy contests have used the internet to communicate their views. Websites used in proxy contests typically post proxy materials, press releases and letters. On a few occasions, stockholders have opposed management initiatives online without soliciting proxies.

Conference calls for analysts

Many companies are using telephone conference calls to alert financial analysts and institutional investors of developments in their company. Top management also answers questions put forward by analysts. This saves a lot of costs as well as time. Analysts from any part of the world can call the telephone number provided by the company and gain information about the company. Since analysts need not be present in a particular venue, travelling is eliminated and thus substantial cost savings are achieved.

Annual reports on CD-ROMs

Another area of technological advance by companies has been the use of CD-ROMs for providing annual reports to its stockholders. Annual reports on CD-ROMs can employ search tools and display video and audio information. However, the main obstacle to using CD-ROM annual reports is the cost of production and high mailing costs. Moreover, with internet usage becoming widely accepted, both investors and companies prefer to access the internet.

In conclusion, technological advances and automation cannot be avoided. Technology has made it possible for everyone to access the stock market freely. Investors sitting in one part of the world can trade on the equity market in another part of the world. They need not even contact the local broker-dealer but can trade directly on the automated trading systems. They can trade almost 24 hours a day, 365 days a year. Investors can gain information on any company located at any part of the world through their website, and can also participate in teleconferences from the luxury of their home and cast telephone votes. Moreover, developments in technology have also reduced trading costs and chances of errors have been reduced. Technology has also pushed down companies' costs. They can raise funds through the internet, reduce costs on media releases and also make it convenient for their global stockholders to have free access to information from their websites.

What is Best Execution?

The concept of best execution differs from execution to execution. For the buyer, best execution would mean the buyer buys at the lowest possible price and for the seller, best execution means the seller sells at the highest possible price. Ideally, best execution should be the one in which the buying price and the selling price match each other. But technically such an ideal situation does not happen in reality.

Not very transparent deal

Best execution in reality will be the price at which a broker-trader executes the trade and not at the best price possible. In the case of a bulk order being placed in the market, the broker-trader may split up the entire order into smaller lots and square off the deal. It is also possible that the broker-trader may execute the smaller lots in different trading systems. In this case, while the actual investor may get a consolidated price for his/her deal, the broker-dealer gains a higher margin on the deal. However, for the investor, the deal is not very transparent as the investor is unaware at what rate his/her deal was actually executed. But for the broker-trader, this deal may have been executed as per "best execution" strategy.

Internalization reduces the chances of best execution

Moreover, with the growth of the ATSs and ECNs, the internalization of trades by broker-traders is on the rise. When a limit order is placed by the investor and the broker-trader may have information that the stock has the potential to rise soon, the broker-trader may internalize the trade and just pass on the limit price to the investor. In this case too, the execution is not as per best execution strategy.

For broker-traders, the best price is that which covers all costs

As there are no standard execution costs, broker-traders try to maximize returns. A broker-trader can only charge minimal brokerage fees to clients. But the expenses for broker-traders are quite high if one considers the investments that have to be made and the wide-ranging services that they provide to their clients for which they cannot charge. Moreover, broker-traders do not operate as charities and therefore have to cover all the costs incurred by them. When they internalize a deal, they are investing their funds, for which they have to get higher returns. In this sense, best execution for broker traders is where they are able to cover all costs.

In conclusion, best execution is not just a price but a process. It is difficult to define different prices quoted for different types of order, different needs for immediacy, different portfolio weightings and so on. As there is no such thing as the same best price for every client or every order, best execution is better addressed as best practice by market participants.

Where Next for Exchanges?

Technology has driven down the costs of trading and exchanges have been forced to cut their transaction fees

The increased use of technology reduces the dependence of investors on stock exchanges for trading activities. Historically, stock exchanges earned their revenues from membership fees, listing and trading fees, clearing and settlement and the provision of market data. Improved technology does away with the requirement of exchange membership and listing fees. Investors trading on the ATSs or ECNs do not need to be members of the trading system. Moreover, with the emerging trend of demutualization of exchanges, this source of revenue is likely to be short-lived. Companies do not need to pay any listing fees for trading on ATSs or ECNs. Moreover, the trading fees are also minimal. This makes the alternative trading systems a better alternative to the exchange.

In the above scenario, the exchange can only charge for market data – price and information on the company. However, for the exchange to be able to command a premium for this data, it will have to give additional information from other sources like the trading price on the alternative trading systems or other exchanges.

This trend will force exchanges to become more efficient by driving down transaction costs and providing better liquidity. Technological advancement has ensured that transaction costs can be cut drastically. With the emerging competition from alternative trading systems and other newer exchanges, most existing exchanges will have to drastically reduce transaction costs.

Ensuring liquidity in the market is essential for retaining exchanges' business …

The efficient execution of a deal is important but providing liquidity is even more important. Liquidity will remain the vital factor for an exchange to remain in business. Unless exchanges are able to provide liquidity in the market, business will be elusive. To attract participants on their trading systems, stock exchanges will have to improve connectivity and message protocol standards to allow the maximum number of participants, including life insurance companies and pension funds, access to the stock exchanges in a cost-effective manner. Exchanges will also need to make customer access and membership as simple as possible, so that all types of participants are able to connect inexpensively.

… and cross-border business expansion …

Another area in which exchanges can look forward to an expansion in their business is in offering remote membership. Remote membership will continue to grow as exchanges look to cross-border business expansion by adding non-local players. Exchanges will also need to formulate new membership issues for these new cross-border members. Cross-border memberships will expand the liquidity of the market.

... and an efficient
clearing and settlement
system

A further area of development for stock exchanges to increase business will be ensuring the efficient clearing and settlement of trades. With technological advances, most exchanges have been able to complete the process very quickly. If stock exchanges are able to complete the entire process – of trading, clearing and settlement – within a day, volumes on the exchange can be expected to grow further.

Most stock exchanges have separate trading and clearing systems for cash and derivatives trading. Exchanges which have been able to develop a single trading and clearing system for both cash and derivatives trading will be able to profit from greater economies of scale. Moreover, these exchanges will be able to spread their costs and risks in the current volatile trading environment.

In conclusion, the key area for the survival of exchanges is to provide an efficient, low-cost trading system, ensure liquidity in the market and develop a fully automatic clearing and settlement system.

CHAPTER 3

The Future of Exchanges

With the advent of technological changes in the trading sphere, exchanges have also evolved. Although their importance as the location where buyers and sellers meet to transact has been reduced drastically with the introduction of alternative trading mechanisms, stock exchanges have continued to function. Trading floors have been abandoned in favor of an electronic interface in some stock exchanges, but not others. The internet has transformed the brokerage business, but has had little impact so far on IPOs. Greater international competition among exchanges has put increasing pressure on regulators to regulate more efficiently or face the prospect of regulating an increasingly irrelevant fragment of the securities industry.

Recent technological advances will create a natural monopoly of the bigger exchanges. According to Ruben Lee of the Oxford Finance Group (UK), trading will be concentrated among a small number of exchanges. However, he believes that network externalities are important and concedes that they may not be all powerful and thus it is possible that the number of exchanges may proliferate simply because automated exchanges are so cheap to operate.

Changes in Stock Exchanges

Historically, stock exchanges have, of necessity, been physical places where traders met and negotiated transactions face to face. Traders worked to regulate themselves and enhance investor confidence in the integrity of markets. Membership fees rationed access to these early exchanges, where space was limited. High volume traders chose to become members in order to take advantage of the ability to buy and sell in liquid markets and, in turn, become intermediaries for other market participants.

The economics of automated trading are undermining this traditional exchange model. An exchange no longer needs be a physical place and so it is no longer necessary to ration access, as the marginal cost of an additional member is almost zero. In future, exchanges will no longer rely on membership fee revenue, but instead will find that trade data may prove to be an exchange's most valuable asset. Exchanges will behave like media companies and attempt to charge for the provision of information. According to Ruben Lee, when the exchanges lose their importance in the listing, trading and clearing functions due to techno-logical advances, exchanges will seek to control and exploit the intellectual property in the price and quote data arising from their trading systems.

These changes in the trading atmosphere have made global stock exchanges rethink their business strategy and find ways of how best to survive. In the process, exchanges have evolved new corporate, legal and business models to strengthen governance and chal-lenge the competition. This process of transformation from members' associations into for-profit corpora-tions is referred to as "demutualization".

Demutualization of Exchanges

Demutualization refers to the change in legal status of the exchange from a mutual association with one vote per member (and possibly consensus-based decision making) to a company limited by shares, with one vote per share (with majority-based decision making). Demutualization makes sense if it induces a change in the exchange's objective from managing the interests of a closed member-based organization with a central focus on providing services for the benefit primarily of the members/brokers and keeping costs and investments limited to financing agreed by members, into a company set up with the objective of maximizing the value of the equity shares by focusing on generating profits from servicing the demands of its customers (brokers and investors) in a competitive manner.

The number of stock exchanges that have been privatized or listed has been increasing since the Stockholm Stock Exchange demutualized in 1993. Currently, of a total of 230 exchanges worldwide, 25 exchanges are demutualized and listed.

Factors Driving the Demutualization of Exchanges

With the widespread proliferation of ATSs and ECNs, exchanges are no longer the sole primary and secondary market makers or sole service providers of trade execution. ATSs and ECNs have allowed efficient and effective matching of the buy and sell orders of customers at lower transaction costs, while offering price transparency, trader anonymity and extended trading hours. Large global brokers are able to internalize their own order stock and only report the net position as a trade to the stock exchange and thus avoid transaction costs.

The transformation of exchanges from mutual to demutualized structure involves two key features:

- A change in the ownership structure

- A change in legal as well as organizational form.

Both need to be accompanied by adequate safeguards to ensure appropriate governance.

Ownership Structure

The transformation from the mutual member-based to demutualized exchange involves issues of transferability of ownership from members to non-members. There are various ways that dilution of membership can be achieved. Sequentially, it involves the conversion of existing member seats by monetizing these and assigning a certain value per seat. Once the valuation is done, members can opt to convert their membership to share ownership or sell off their interests to non-members. In most cases of demutualization of exchanges, members have opted to retain their share ownership. A listing of equity shares in the exchange facilitates the unlocking of the members' equity and the buyout of the interest of the traders, while leading to the monetization of the value of members' seats. An entity with freely transferable shares, rather than membership rights, can form equity swap-based strategic alliances or mergers with other exchanges, domestically or in other countries or time zones. Such alliances are stronger and offer greater creditability than pure cooperation agreements.

Legal and Organizational Form

To avoid stock exchanges operating in special or limited interests, regulators of the exchange industry often place restrictions on ownership by one holder or a group of holders to non-controlling stakes of 5–10 percent. Limits on ownership stakes could affect potential takeovers by other exchanges. Such takeovers could be advantageous especially if the takeover is by an efficient exchange of an inefficient or not so efficient exchange. A better exchange can, by taking over a weaker exchange, significantly improve the functioning of the latter. Recognizing the synergies of takeover, most demutualized exchanges have provisions to allow other exchanges, or technology partners, the possibility of acquiring or swapping strategic stakes. The reluctance to relinquish control to strategic partners or owners remains one reason why non-equity, swap-based cooperative alliances have been more prolific in the exchange industry. Several hostile takeover attempts (including OM Gruppen's moves to acquire the LSE in 2000 and the bidding war for the Sydney Futures Exchange by the Australian Stock Exchange and Computershare in 1999) have failed due to the voting strength still exerted by brokers.

The legal structure for demutualized exchanges is based on considerations similar to those for any profit-making company, including decisions on the number of stockholders (partnership vs. corporation), voting procedures, limitation of liability (liability limited to equity invested vs. joint and several liability for all debts), accounting and reporting requirements (based on taxation laws and on partners/shareholders' access to information on the company) and distribution of dividends.

Benefits of Demutualization

Improvements in corporate governance

When exchanges are run as mutual associations, member brokers have the exclusive right to trade on the trading platforms and also derive profits from the intermediation of non-member broker transactions. Member brokers resist changes as these entail additional costs leading to loss of revenue. Moreover, on many occasions, in order to control the monopoly of member brokers, the government of the country has to appoint its own officials to mitigate entrenched vested interests. In the long run, appointing such officials may prove detrimental to the growth of the stock exchange.

Under demutualization, there is an increased acceptance of the separation of ownership from membership that automatically provides trading rights. This segregation helps to introduce effective corporate governance if:

■ There are accompanying improvements in the incentive structure which allow exchanges to sell their equity stakes to non-member brokers and outsiders.

■ Decision making is based on this new ownership structure (not on rights of intermediation).

■ There is effective oversight of a governing board and a company structure.

Once the exchanges are demutualized, some exchanges have granted less than 50 percent of the voting rights to the broker members on the board of the exchange. To gradually reduce broker member influence on the board, exchanges have appointed independent directors or directors who are non-trading owners.

Functions of the management of demutualized exchanges	The management of the exchange has to be under qualified personnel who are motivated to act not only in the best interest of the stockholders, but also to conduct the business in a prudent manner so as not to disrupt the orderly and fair trading in the capital markets. The management is accountable to the board, which determines the management's appointment and remuneration, supervises the strategic direction and audits the financial and operational results, including risk management, and, if required, effects the removal of the management. To ensure the effective supervision and auditing of management, the majority of the board members should be truly independent directors.
Regulation necessary for good corporate governance of exchanges	To remain competitive, a stock exchange must follow international best practices in ethics and procedures. This is necessary in order to ensure that institutional investors do not shift their investments to other alternatives perceived to be more fair or secure. Therefore, it is in the profit motivated exchange's best interest to ensure fair and transparent practices, and, as such, good corporate governance needs to be an integral part of the exchange once it is driven by the profit motive.

Integration and Consolidation of Stock Exchanges

	Many exchanges in Europe and Asia have recently consolidated to increase their volume of business, while reducing costs through the integration of operations. But the early integrations can be traced back to the twentieth century in the USA.
Consolidation of American stock exchanges	In the early twentieth century, there were dozens of regional exchanges in the US – apart from the NYSE, the American Stock Exchange (Amex) and the National Association of Securities Dealers (NASD) –

that mainly traded the stock of local companies. However, the industry structure began to change with the introduction of new communication technologies. The emergence of cross-country telephone services after 1915, the coast-to-coast availability of NYSE stock tickers after the mid-1920s and the development of the open-end teletype after 1935 eliminated geographical barriers, allowing the NYSE to capture a large portion of the regional stock exchanges trading volumes.

New regulations in the wake of the 1929 stock market crash were another major factor affecting the industry structure. In 1936, the US Congress granted exchanges "unlisted trading privileges", permitting an exchange to trade any security that was approved for listing on another exchange (Securities and Exchange Commission 1944). Unlisted trading privileges facilitated the trading of a single stock on multiple exchanges.

Due to these technological and regulatory changes, the percentage of "regional-only" stocks traded on regional exchanges declined drastically, while the number of stocks that traded simultaneously on multiple exchanges increased rapidly, leading to intense competition among stock exchanges for order flows. Investors could choose the exchange for their order execution based on the cost of execution, speed of execution and quality of execution.

This competition among exchanges led to the consolidation of various exchanges. Many smaller exchanges decided to merge. First mover advantages were beneficial to these exchanges, compelling further consolidation among the other exchanges. This consolidation not only benefited the investors by way of lower trading fees but also benefited the exchanges. With more investors flocking to a particular exchange, the exchange also commanded higher respect. This in turn led to higher values for the membership of that particular exchange. However, since the technological and regulatory changes did not take place overnight, consolidation proved to be a gradual process.

The consolidation process in Europe

With the formation of the European Union (EU), cross-border trading among European exchanges is becoming popular. The introduction of the euro and a wider acceptance of equity as a financing tool are encouraging investors in Europe to engage in more cross-border transactions in search of profit-making opportunities. Yet despite the appeal of cross-border trading, most stock exchanges in Europe are national institutions that trade only local, country-specific stocks.

However, this market structure is changing, albeit on a slower scale. Several ambitious initiatives have been undertaken to create, through mergers or other consolidations, pan-European exchanges that offer trading in stocks from many European countries. The two most prominent exchanges that have been formed through mergers are the Euronext and OMX.

The OMX operates the exchanges in Copenhagen, Stockholm, Helsinki, Tallinn, Riga and Vilnius (Lithuania) (all exchanges owned by OMX), as well as the stock exchanges in Oslo and Iceland. It operates the common trading platform SAXESS across these exchanges. It provides customer benefits, such as harmonized Nordic and Baltic trading rules as well as one access point to the eight different markets. As at end May 2005, the OMX exchange has 677 companies listed on it and 144 trading members.

In another consolidation, the Paris Bourse, the Amsterdam exchange and the Brussels exchange merged in

March 2000 to form Euronext – the integrated European stock exchange. Although the different jurisdictions and local licenses of the individual exchanges are maintained, Euronext provides a single operating umbrella for all three exchanges. Trading is centralized, and a uniform trading platform – the Paris Bourse's NSC trading engine – is used, allowing a single trade price to be established. Shares are listed at a national level and companies can select their trading venue from among the three exchanges.

The consolidation process in Asia

In Asia, exchanges have opted for a merger among the various smaller domestic exchanges. They have also built alliances by establishing cross-border linkages with other exchanges within or outside the region. Emphasis has been largely to regroup businesses to broaden the markets, offer issuers and investors better distribution networks and improve liquidity. Predominant mergers within the country have taken place in Singapore, Hong Kong, Australia, Japan and Kuala Lumpur. Most of the dominant exchanges in the Asia-Pacific regions have established cross-border trading relationships both within the region as well as with European and American exchanges. These exchanges are also implementing integrated trading and settlement infrastructures to facilitate STP.

Advantages of Consolidation

The consolidation of stock exchanges leads to important benefits for the financial sector. In general, stock exchanges have shown greater economies of scale both in operations as well as in trading if they are consolidated. Moreover, the exchanges benefit from operational economies of scale by implementing a shared trading platform which in turn can increase trading liquidity and thereby reduce market fragmentation.

Compatible or shared trading platforms

The consolidation of stock exchanges could give rise to compatible trading platforms, eliminating the need for investment in different trading systems. An exchange incurs substantial fixed costs to develop, upgrade and operate its trading system. Because such systems often have a similar basic architecture, a merger of exchanges – or the sharing of a common trading platform among several exchanges – would enhance efficiency.

In addition, common or shared trading platforms could benefit investment banks and brokers that engage in cross-border transactions. These institutions currently face significant access costs to maintain connections with a variety of trading systems. In this respect, a consolidation of stock exchanges could lead to a greater standardization of the trading formats used by the financial services industry. It would be more efficient for institutional investors and broker-traders to connect to a limited number of stock exchanges, rather than to a large number of small local stock exchanges with incompatible formats.

Increases liquidity

The compatibility of trading platforms reduces the cost of cross-border transactions, attracting new investors to the equity markets and generating higher trading volumes. Higher trading volumes are important for an exchange as they increase the liquidity of the market. Moreover, new innovative products can be introduced when the market sphere is bigger. By encouraging new equity investment, the consolidation of exchanges could lead to greater market liquidity.

Reduced market fragmentation

Parallel trading of the same security on different national exchanges contributes to the fragmentation of financial markets. The creation of a common trading platform resolves this problem. Under such a system, all buy and sell orders could be funneled through a small number of major exchanges, thereby concentrating, rather than fragmenting, order flows. Greater price stability and more precise price discovery could result from concentrated order flows.

Barriers to Consolidation

Despite the potential benefits of consolidation, several forces are working against the rapid consolidation of exchanges. These are product differentiation, the existence of cross-country legal and regulatory differences, high information costs and the widespread fragmentation of clearing and settlement systems.

Product differentiation

The potential economies of scale that a single stock exchange can give do not necessarily mean that one such venue represents the most efficient market structure. Investors and companies may prefer to be served by a number of smaller exchanges that offer distinct products and target diverse clients. The differentiation of services can allow several exchanges to operate side by side despite any scale economies brought by a single market.

Legal and regulatory differences

Cross-country legal and regulatory differences may also hinder consolidation. Each country will have its own set of rules. Disparities in national rules discourage cross-border trading because investors and companies must familiarize themselves with the regulatory regimes of various countries.

Moreover, accounting norms also differ from country to country. Tax treatment will also vary from country to country. Besides, to increase local investment, the governments of individual countries may have imposed certain policies which favor home investment.

Information costs

Information costs increase when there is cross-border trading and investors are always price conscious while trading. Investors often find that cultural and linguistic differences, along with the geographic distance between home and foreign markets, make access to information on foreign securities more difficult and expensive to obtain. In fact, information costs are a key reason why investors exhibit home country bias despite the advantages of international portfolio diversification.

Fragmentation of clearing and settlement systems

Fragmented clearing and settlement systems also stand in the way of consolidation. After a trade has been executed, clearing take place, that is, the buyer and seller confirm the terms of the trade, and the clearing agency calculates the counterparty obligations. Settlement entails the actual transfer of funds and asset ownership between buyer and seller. Unlike trade execution, which occurs at exchanges, clearing and settlement can be completed at agencies that are either independent or controlled by an exchange.

There are numerous clearing and settlement organizations that are sharply divided along national lines. Such fragmentation, which brings with it numerous clearing and settlement processes, can result in significantly higher transaction costs.

Due to these factors, although consolidation appears technically to be a good concept, adoption is taking longer to come about. However, most global exchanges are trying to make the regulatory system uniform or similar to the practices in well-established exchanges. If the clearing and settlement systems are integrated with uniform procedures, the consolidation of exchanges can happen more quickly.

Going forward, governments can play an important role in the transformation of their individual countries' stock exchanges. They could facilitate the consolidation process by fostering competition for order flows among exchanges rather than following protectionist strategies. Competition could be promoted by encouraging regulatory standardization across stock markets and allowing more liberalized trading of stocks on multiple venues. The ensuing benefits will be passed on to investors and companies in the form of improved financial services, decreased transaction expenses and reduced costs of obtaining capital.

However, at this point it would not be presumptuous to assume that the global stock exchange industry will be dominated by a few trading exchanges, with fully integrated clearing and settlement systems and a unified accounting and regulatory system. This may not happen overnight and may take a decade or two. But the end result of this evolution will be that a handful of exchanges will control the global cash and derivatives market, using STP technology for the trading, clearing and settlement of traded products. Just visualize this – an investor from Beijing may be trading on an exchange product listed in Europe but traded on an exchange in Australia. Despite the distance, the entire transaction will close within seconds and his account at Beijing will be simultaneously debited.

New Products

As time passes, existing trading instruments become the norm and trading volumes stagnate. To increase volume and attract new clients, financial engineers develop new products. Some new products are slight variations of existing products and some are totally new products. The new products that have been introduced in recent times are variations in derivatives products as well as other newer products like exchange-traded funds (ETFs), single stock futures (SSFs) and covered warrants. This development is expected to continue and in the coming years we can expect many more such new trading products in the financial industry.

Exotic Derivative Options

The derivatives covered in Chapter 1 are termed *plain vanilla* products. They have standard, well-defined properties and trade actively. Their prices or implied volatilities are quoted by exchanges or broker-traders on a regular basis. One of the exciting aspects of the over-the-counter derivatives market is the number of non-standard or *exotic* products that have been created by financial engineers. Although they are usually a relatively small part of a portfolio, these are becoming increasingly important as they are generally more profitable than plain vanilla products.

Exotic products have evolved for a number of reasons:

■ Sometimes they meet a genuine hedging need in the market.

- Sometimes there are tax, accounting, legal or regulatory reasons.

- Sometimes the products are designed to reflect a corporate treasurer's view of potential future movements in particular market variables.

- Occasionally an exotic product is developed by an investment bank to appear more attractive than it is to an unwary corporate treasurer.

A few of the exotic options are discussed below.

Non-standard American Options

In a standard American option, exercise can take place any time during the life of the option and the exercise price remains the same. But in a non-standard American option, early exercise may be restricted to certain dates, or early exercise is only possible after an initial "lock-in" period, or the strike price may change during the life of the option.

Forward Start Options

These options will start at some time in the future. They are sometimes used in employee incentive schemes. The terms of the options usually specify that they will be at the money at the time they start.

Compound Options

These are options on options. There are four main types of compound option:

- A call on call

- A put on call

■ A call on a put

■ A put on a put.

Compound options have two strike prices and two exercise dates.

Chooser Options

A chooser option, sometimes referred to as an "as you like it option", has the feature that, after a specified period of time, the holder can choose whether the option is a call or a put.

Barrier Options

These are options where the payoff depends on whether the underlying asset price reaches a certain level during a certain period of time. A number of different types of barrier options are regularly traded on the over-the-counter market. They are attractive to some market participants because they are less expensive than the corresponding regular options. These barrier options can be classified as either "knock-out options" or "knock-in options". A knock-out option ceases to exist when the underlying asset price reaches a certain barrier, while a knock-in option comes into existence only when the underlying asset price reaches a barrier.

Binary Options

These are options with discontinuous payoffs. An example of a binary option is a cash-or-nothing call option. This pays off nothing if the asset price ends up below the strike price and pays an equal amount to the asset price itself if it ends up above the strike price.

Lookback Options

The payoffs from lookback options depend on the maximum or minimum asset price reached during the life of the option. A lookback call is the way that the holder can buy the underlying asset at the lowest price achieved during the life of the option. Similarly, a lookback put is the way that the holder can sell the underlying asset at the highest price achieved during the life of the option. The underlying asset in a lookback option is often a commodity.

Shout Options

A shout option is a European option where the holder can "shout" to the writer at one time during its life. At the end of the life of the option, the option holder receives either the usual payoff from a European option or the intrinsic value at the time of the shout, whichever is greater.

Asian Options

Asian options are options where the payoff depends on the average price of the underlying asset during at least some part of the life of the option.

Options to Exchange One Asset for Another

These options are sometimes referred to as exchange options. An option to buy yen with Australian dollars is, from the point of view of a US investor, an option to exchange one foreign currency asset for another foreign currency asset. A stock tender offer is an option to exchange shares in one stock for shares in another stock.

Basket Options

This is an option where the payoff is dependent on the value of a portfolio (or basket) of assets. The assets are usually either individual stocks or stock indices or currencies.

The above options are a few exotic options being traded in the financial markets. However, before trading an exotic option, it is important for institutional investors to assess not only how it should be priced but also the difficulties that are likely to be experienced in hedging it. Exotic options sometimes prove to be easier to hedge using the underlying asset than the corresponding plain vanilla option. In general, Asian options are easier to hedge because the payoff becomes progressively more certain as they approach maturity.

An alternative approach that can be used to hedge a position in exotic options is "static options replication". This involves searching for a portfolio of actively traded options that approximately replicate the option position. The basic principle underlying static options replication is as follows. If two portfolios are worth the same on a certain boundary, they are also worth the same at all interior points of the boundary.

Exchange-traded Funds

An exchange-traded fund (ETF) is a type of investment company whose investment objective is to achieve the same return as a particular market index. An ETF is similar to an index fund in that it will primarily invest in the securities of companies that are included in a selected market index. An ETF will invest in either all the securities or a representative sample of the securities included in the index.

Although ETFs are legally classified as open-end companies or unit investment trusts (UITs), they differ from traditional open-end companies and UITs in the following respects:

■ ETFs do not sell individual shares directly to investors and only issue their shares in large blocks (for example blocks of 50,000 shares) that are known as "creation units".

■ Investors generally do not purchase creation units with cash. Instead they buy creation units with a basket of securities that generally mirrors the ETF's portfolio. Those who purchase creation units are frequently institutions.

■ After purchasing a creation unit, an investor splits it up and sells the individual shares on a secondary market. This permits other investors to purchase individual shares (instead of creation units).

■ Investors who want to sell their ETF shares have two options:
1 They can sell individual shares to other investors in the secondary market.
2 They can sell the creation units back to the ETF. In addition, ETFs generally redeem creation units by giving investors the securities that comprise the portfolio instead of cash. This can be illustrated through the following example. Suppose an ETF invested in the stocks contained in the Dow Jones Industrial Average (DJIA) would give a redeeming shareholder the actual securities that constitute the DJIA instead of cash. Because of the limited scope of redeeming the ETF shares,

ETFs are not considered to be – and may not call themselves – mutual funds.

An ETF, like any other type of investment company, will have a prospectus. All investors that purchase creation units receive a prospectus. Some ETFs also deliver a prospectus to secondary market purchasers. ETFs that do not deliver a prospectus are required to give investors a document known as a product description, which summarizes key information about the ETF. ETFs that are legally structured as open-end companies (but not those that are structured as UITs) must also have statements of additional information (SAI). Open-end ETFs (but not UIT ETFs) must provide shareholders with annual and semi-annual reports.

How Does an ETF Function?

ETFs are securities certificates that state the legal right of ownership over a part of a basket of individual stock certificates. Several different kinds of financial firms are needed for ETFs to come into being, trade at prices that closely match their underlying assets, and offload when investors no longer want them. The fund manager is responsible for all the groundwork. He/she is the main backer behind any ETF, and he/she must submit a detailed plan on the functioning of the ETF to the securities regulatory authority of the country.

In theory, the fund manager has to establish clear procedures and describe precisely the composition of the ETF to the other firms involved in the creation and redemption of the ETF. In practice, however, only the biggest institutional money management firms with experience in indexing tend to play this role. These money management firms direct pension funds with enormous baskets of stocks in markets all over the world to loan stocks necessary for the creation process. They also create demand by lining up customers, either institutional or retail, to buy a newly introduced ETF.

The creation of an ETF officially begins with an authorized participant, who is also referred to as a "market maker" or specialist. These participants assemble the appropriate basket of stocks and send them to a specially designated custodial bank for safekeeping. These baskets are normally quite large, sufficient to purchase 10,000–50,000 shares of the ETF in question.

The custodial bank holds the basket of stocks in the fund's account for the fund manager to monitor. The flow of individual stocks and ETF certificates are kept with the CSD which records individual stock sales and keeps the official record of these transactions. It records ETF transfer of title just like any other stock. It provides an extra layer of assurance against fraud.

Once the authorized participant obtains the ETF from the custodial bank, it is free to sell it into the open market. From then on ETF shares are sold and resold freely among investors on the open market.

Redemption is simply the reverse. An authorized participant buys a large block of ETFs on the open market and sends it to the custodial bank and in return receives an equivalent basket of individual stocks which are then sold on the open market or typically returned to their loanees.

What is the Motivation for the Fund Managers to Perform Efficiently?

All intermediaries in this transaction chain are rewarded for good performance. Fund managers get a small portion of the fund's annual assets as their fees. Similarly, the investors who loan stocks to make up a basket get an interest fee for the favor. The custodial bank also gets a management fee from the fund manager. The authorized participant is primarily driven by the profit margins from the difference in price between the basket of stocks and the ETF and on part of the bid-ask spread of the ETF itself.

Although the process appears cumbersome, the entire process is quite transparent. Everyone can clearly observe what goes into an ETF, investor fees are clearly laid out and investors are confident that they can exit at any time. Even the authorized participants have modest but assured returns.

Why Should One Invest in ETFs?

Low trading fees

ETFs are economical to buy and also to maintain over the long run. These are attractive for the typical buy and hold investor. The annual trading fees of ETFs are also low compared to trading fees for mutual fund products.

Flexible trading

ETFs differ fundamentally from traditional mutual funds. Mutual funds do not allow trading in mid-session. Traditional mutual funds take the order of their investors in the morning session, but the transaction is actually executed at the close of the market. The price that an investor in a mutual fund receives is that of the closing session of that particular trading day. However, this is not so for an ETF. The ETFs trade throughout the day and allow investors to lock in a price for the underlying stocks immediately. Moreover, no penalties or back-end fees are levied when the ETFs are redeemed.

Best performance expected due to joint responsibility

The ETFs are considered as safe as the underlying share certificates they represent. Internally, the ETFs are more complex entities than mutual funds. A combination of players – brokers, money managers and market specialists – are all responsible for the operation of the ETFs. Since all these specialists also have a stake in the profitability of the ETF, their operation of the fund is smoother.

Tax efficiency

When a mutual fund is faced with shareholder redemptions, it must sell the underlying securities to raise the cash to pay shareholders. Any capital gains that are triggered by those transactions are passed on to the other shareholders. Because shareholders sell shares to others, ETFs do not have to sell underlying securities to meet redemptions. However, as their underlying benchmarks change periodically, ETFs may have to pay out distributions. In general though, distributions should happen less often with ETFs than with traditional mutual funds.

Global product

ETFs can be bought and sold in any country in the world.

Cash efficient

Since ETFs don't need to maintain a cash position to satisfy redemptions, they can be fully invested in securities. This usually allows them to outperform a mutual fund with a corresponding basket of securities, which incurs a substantial cash drag.

| Sophisticated hedging options | Because ETFs can be bought on margin or sold short like a stock, they allow experienced investors to implement sophisticated hedging, market-neutral, and other alternative investment strategies. |

Despite the above advantages of investing in ETFs, there are a few disadvantages too.

| Payment of multiple brokerages | Every time an investor buys or sells an ETF, the investor has to pay a brokerage commission. For investors who are frequently changing the basket of ETFs, these multiple brokerage costs could offset the lower annual costs that ETFs usually charge. |

| Bid/ask spread issues | Because of the way ETFs are structured, you could end up buying an ETF at a premium to the portfolio's value and selling at a discount. Although this is not very common, it can happen if the stock is thinly traded. Moreover, in volatile markets the bid or ask spreads may widen and consequently eat into the margins. |

| Inefficient matching | When the market has a low liquidity with low trading volumes, it may be difficult to match an ETF seller with an ETF buyer. In such a circumstance, spreads may widen and the transaction may not be executed. |

However, despite the above disadvantages, ETFs are currently all the rage in most economies. Most institutional investors prefer to invest in ETFs over the traditional mutual funds. Institutional investors structure their portfolios efficiently and allocate a different proportion of their funds for different sectors. By using the ETFs that track a particular underlying market segment, institutional investors are able to execute their strategy more effectively than actively managed mutual funds.

Single Stock Futures

Single stock futures (SSFs) are futures contracts on individual stocks. SSFs are an agreement between two parties that commits one party to buy a stock and another to sell a stock at a given price and on a specified date. SSFs are exchange-traded contracts based on an underlying stock. They are similar to existing futures contracts for gold, crude oil, bonds and stock indexes. The price movement of the SSF is based on the underlying stock that it is tied to. As the price of the stock goes up and down, so too does the stock future. However, the actual stockholders have voting rights and are also eligible for dividends. The SSF holders do not have voting rights and are not eligible for voting as they are not holders of the actual stock.

Single stock futures are a way to reap the benefits of a stock's performance without actually owning the stock. Theoretically they offer the benefits of ownership, of leveraging the stock or its underlying assets.

Why Should One Invest in SSFs?

The following are some of the key benefits of SSFs.

Easier and cheaper to initiate a short position

An SSF short sale is likely to be done at a superior price because most futures trade at a premium to the stock price. Selling short in the futures market is quicker as there is less hassle with borrowing shares.

Cheaper to leverage long positions

Trading of an SSF requires significantly lower margins. This improves the cash flow position of investors as they require lower funds to buy an SSF contract than actually purchasing the stock. Retail investors will therefore save interest costs, making the leveraged long position more affordable with futures than stocks.

Improved cash flow	Since trading SSFs requires lower margins, investors can use the balance of funds with them to purchase some other products. This improves the liquidity of the market. Moreover, interest charges on the broker loan rates are usually higher than the interest rates embedded in the pricing structure of futures. This means a saving by way of interest costs to the investors. This interest saving provides improved cash flow to the investor.
Cleaner hedge than options	Price movements in SSFs are in tandem with the price movement of the intrinsic stocks. This results in the SSF price moving with the price movements of the underlying stock. As the stock price moves up, so does the value of the SSF. This helps the SSFs to provide a cleaner hedge than options (prices of which do not move in tandem with the underlying stock) and investors prefer to use SSFs for the hedging of stocks.
Reduced foreign exchange risk	Since only a nominal margin is required to buy an SSF, foreign investors can keep more of their money in the currency of their residence and thus minimize the impact of currency volatility on their portfolio. Moreover, the ability to control a stock without full payment allows foreign investors to reduce foreign exchange risk.
Additional trading strategies	SSFs make accessible additional investment strategies like hedging, spread trading and leveraging. These strategies are not so readily available to investors if they use other trading products.

Hedging

Hedging refers to placing a futures trade that is opposite to an existing stock position. The hedge neutralizes the risk of the existing position. An example of this is that if an investor is holding shares of ABC Company, he/she can sell ABC futures as a hedge against the position he/she holds.

The hedge allows an investor to leave the original position in place while neutralizing the risk. The investor postpones a taxable stock sale and continues to receive dividends from his or her stockholdings.

Because of the convenience of using futures, the decision to place a hedge can be a simple one for an investor. Since there is no restriction for the investor to maintain the hedge for a specific period, some hedgers trade around their positions. This means that the investors can place and remove the hedge many times over the life of the position.

Spread Trading

A spread trade involves holding both long and short positions in stocks that are related in some ways. In SSFs, the spread trade attempts to exploit the positive developments in one company against the negative or neutral developments in a related company. This can be illustrated by the following example. Suppose a pharmaceutical company X has developed a new product which is a stronger than the existing product of pharmaceutical company Y. In this case, pharmaceutical company X will be able to gain a bigger market share and at the same time move into the market share of company Y. For an investor, it is an excellent opportunity to spread his/her trade. The investor will hold a long position in company X and a short position in company Y.

The first step in placing a spread is determining the spread ratio. The spread ratio is simply a means to equalize the investment in two stocks. The goal is to find the ratio where a given percentage move in one stock will equate to an equal dollar move in the other stock. The spread ratio is calculated by dividing the value of one stock by the value of the other.

Leveraged Trading

Leveraged trading means that the investor does not need to put the entire value of the stock for purchasing the stock. In SSFs, the investor has to make payment for only the margin required to hold the SSF. If the investor uses borrowed funds for buying the SSF, he/she will need to borrow a lower amount and consequently pay lower interest charges. Even if the investor is using personal funds, he/she needs to block a lower portion of his/her funds on the SSF. Due to this lower margin requirement, SSFs always trade slightly higher than the actual current stock price.

However, leverage is a double-edged sword. It can also work against the investor. Since futures margins are very low, an adverse price move can mean that an investor will need to send more money in response to an increase in margin call. Moreover, in futures, the investor faces the additional risk of being forced out of his/her position. This is when the investor is not able to send additional money fast enough during a margin call. It is therefore evident that the benefits of higher leverage can become a disadvantage to an undercapitalized investor.

ETF Futures

ETF futures are future contracts on exchange-traded funds. The ETFs have been successful in generating business with high trading volumes and strong retail interest. Over the years the ETFs have witnessed rapid growth in the funds under management. Due to the overwhelming success of the ETFs, the exchanges felt the need to introduce a futures contract on the ETFs.

Just as in any futures contract, the ETF futures contract can also be acquired at a marginal cost as compared to the underlying ETF. Moreover, currently all listed ETF futures settle through physical delivery, whereas the index futures settle in cash. In other words, a trader who holds one of these contracts through expiration will receive 100 shares of the underlying fund. As a result, ETF futures have a potential advantage for traders who want to maintain exposure to the underlying index after expiration.

Another characteristic is that there tends to be a slight difference between the price of the ETF shares and the price of the underlying index. This tracking error makes the ETF futures a better match than the index future for someone hedging a position in the underlying ETF shares.

However, there is also a structural disadvantage in using the ETF futures contract. As a security future, ETF futures are subject to a minimum margin of 20 percent, whereas index futures are usually margined at a lower percentage. Therefore the index futures will be more attractive for market participants seeking the maximum leverage. Another disadvantage of the ETF future is that the uptick rule, which hinders short sales of stock, does not apply to ETFs, which removes a potential incentive for short sellers to use the future.

Covered Warrants

A covered warrant is an instrument which allows investors to buy or sell an underlying asset at a pre-established price.

Covered warrants are of two types:

- Call warrants allow the investor to buy the underlying asset.
- Put warrants allow the investor to sell the underlying asset.

Covered warrants are generally issued by intermediaries other than the issuer. Most frequently, the underlying asset is represented by shares, but other instruments can also serve as underlyings (bonds, interest rates and so on). At the expiration date, they provide for a cash settlement of the potential gain.

Market Efficiencies

So far we have discussed the trends in the evolution of the stock market since the birth of the first exchange. The trends have been highlighted, the different trading systems have been discussed and the technological evolution and its growing importance have been illustrated. But the reader may want to know – which market is the most efficient or where should an investor trade? An efficient market is one where the security prices fully reflect all relevant information that is available about the fundamental value of the securities. Because a security is a claim on future cash flows, this fundamental value is the present value of the future cash flows that the owner of the security expects to receive. The cash flows anticipated for stocks consist of the stream of expected dividends paid to stockholders plus the expected price of the stock when sold. In the present value calculation, future cash flows are discounted by an interest rate that is a function of the risk of those cash flows. The more risk the cash flows, the higher the rate used in discounting.

Market efficiency does not require that the market price be equal to the true value at every point in time. All it requires is that errors in the market price be unbiased, that is, that the price can be greater than or less than the true value, as long as these deviations are random. The fact that the deviations from true value are random implies, in a rough sense, that there is an equal chance that stocks are under- or overvalued at any point in time, and that these deviations are uncorrelated with any observable variable. For example, in an efficient market, stocks with a lower price–earnings (P/E) ratio should be no more or less likely to be undervalued than stocks with high P/E ratio. If the deviations of market price from true value are random, it follows that no group of investors should be able to constantly find under- or overvalued stocks using any investment strategy.

Market efficiency will differ for different investor groups. While one investor group may think of a particular exchange as inefficient, another investor group may think the same exchange very efficient. Market efficiencies therefore have to be specific not only about the particular market but also about the investor group. It is extremely unlikely that all markets are efficient to all investors, but it is entirely possible that a particular market (for instance the NYSE) is efficient with respect to the average investor. It is also possible that some markets are efficient while others are not, and that a market is efficient with respect to some investors and not to others. This is a direct consequence of differential tax rates and transaction costs, which confer advantages on some investors relative to others.

Market efficiency also depends on the availability of information. It assumes that all information is freely available to all and hence the price of a particular stock is a reflection of a fully transparent market condition. In the strictest sense, market efficiency assumes that all information, public as well as private, is reflected in the market prices and that even investors with precise inside information will be unable to beat the market.

Why Does Informational Efficiency Matter?

The equity markets channel funds from savers to firms, which use the funds to finance projects. Informational efficiency is necessary if funds, allocated through the capital market, are to flow to the highest valued projects. Stockholders want company managements to maximize stock prices and thus will attempt to ensure that their managements undertake projects that will increase the value of their stock. Management compensation packages tied to stock performance are one way in which stockholders align management's interests with their own. However, the maximization of stock prices can result in the capital market directing funds to the most valuable projects only if stocks are efficiently priced, in the sense of accurately reflecting the fundamental value of all future cash flows. Thus, if capital markets are efficient, there is no reason to expect managements to emphasize the short run at the expense of long-term projects. Additionally, efficient markets determine the prices at which existing and potential security holders are willing to exchange claims on a firm's future cash flows.

The study of capital market efficiency examines how much, how fast and how accurately available information is incorporated into security prices. Economists often classify efficiency into three categories based on what is meant as "available information" – the weak, semi-strong and strong forms.

Weak form efficiency

Weak form efficiency exists if security prices fully reflect all the information contained in the history of past prices and returns. (The return is the profit on the security calculated as a percentage of an initial price.) If capital markets are weak form efficient, then investors cannot earn excess profits from trading rules based on past prices or returns. Therefore, stock returns are not predictable, and so-called technical analysis is useless. Under weak form efficiency, some public information about fundamentals may not yet be reflected in prices.

Semi-strong form efficiency

Under semi-strong form efficiency, security prices fully reflect all public information. Thus, only traders with access to non-public information, such as corporate insiders, can earn excess profits.

Strong form efficiency

Finally, under strong form efficiency, all information – even apparent company secrets – is incorporated in security prices, thus, no investor can earn excess profit trading on public or non-public information.

The Efficient Market Hypothesis and the Random Walk Theory

The efficient market hypothesis (EMH) evolved in the 1960s from the PhD dissertation of Eugene Fama.

According to the EMH, at any given time, security prices fully reflect all available information. The implications of the efficient market hypothesis are truly profound. Most individuals who buy and sell securities (stocks in particular) do so under the assumption that the securities they are buying are worth more than the price they are paying, while securities they are selling are worth less than the selling price. But if markets are efficient and current prices fully reflect all information, then buying and selling securities in an attempt to outperform the market will effectively be a game of chance rather than skill.

The random walk theory asserts that price movements will not follow any patterns or trends and that past price movements cannot be used to predict future price movements. Much of the theory on these subjects can be traced to the French mathematician Louis Bachelier, whose PhD dissertation "The Theory of Speculation" (1900) included some remarkable insights and commentary. Bachelier concluded that "The mathematical expectation of the speculator is zero" and he described this condition as a "fair game".

Are Equity Markets Truly Efficient?

The debate about efficient equity markets has resulted in hundreds of empirical studies attempting to determine whether specific markets are in fact "efficient" and, if so, to what degree. Many novice investors are surprised to learn that a tremendous amount of evidence supports the efficient market hypothesis. Early tests on the EMH focused on technical analysis and the role of technical analysts has been challenged by the EMH theory.

Researchers have uncovered numerous anomalies that contradict the efficient market hypothesis. The paradox of efficient markets is that if every investor believed that a market was efficient, then the market would not be efficient because no one would analyze securities. In effect, efficient markets depend on market participants who believe that the market is inefficient and trade securities in an attempt to outperform the market.

In reality, markets are neither perfectly efficient nor completely inefficient. All markets are efficient to a certain extent, some more so than others. Rather than being a black or white issue, market efficiency is more a matter of shades of grey. In markets with substantial impairments of efficiency, more knowledgeable investors can strive to outperform less knowledgeable ones. Government bond markets, for instance, are considered to be extremely efficient. Most researchers consider large capitalization stocks also to be very efficient, while small capitalization stocks and international stocks are considered by some to be less efficient. Venture capital funds do not have fluid and continuous markets and are considered to be less efficient because different participants may have varying amounts and quality of information.

The Integration and Consolidation Process in Clearing and Settlement

Technological innovations and a changing regulatory environment have been the fundamental catalysts behind structural changes in modern financial markets. Technological advances have caused less dependency on physical market locations, thus exposing market participants to an increasingly competitive new environment in domestic markets as well as in the global arena. Equally important is the growing interest among institutional and individual investors in maximizing the positive effects of international portfolio diversification, resulting in a rapid expansion in trading internationally.

Clearing and settlement services are essential requisites of a well-functioning securities market. Clearing involves the process of establishing the respective obligations of the buyer and the seller in a security trade, while settlement comprises the actual transfer of securities from the seller to the buyer. Three types of clearance settlement organizations provide these services: domestic central securities depositories (CSDs), international central securities depositories (ICSDs) and custodians.

The CSD was generally closely connected with the trading, clearing and settlement system in a vertically integrated structure, usually based on common ownership. Services were provided in two layers. The CSD provided clearing, settlement, safekeeping and other services to its settlement members. In turn, some of these members, also called "custodians", provided the same services to end users and offered additional value-added services, such as credit facilities or securities lending services. Finally, central counterparties (CCPs) used to limit the provision of netting facilities to derivatives products.

The above compartmentalized specialized roles of different players are fast vanishing. All market players are seeking to provide new services and reach new markets. Every player has become a potential competitor to all the others. CSDs are establishing links between each other and acting as custodians to one another. Custodians are increasingly providing settlement functions. ICSDs are merging with domestic

CSDs and have started providing credit and securities lending facilities. CCPs are expanding their services to all securities markets.

Clearing and Settlement Structures – Are They Integrated?

The settlement infrastructure has traditionally been most integrated in the US securities markets. The best example is the integration of the operations of the Depository Trust Company (DTC) and the National Securities Clearing Corporation (NSCC) under a common holding company, the Depository Trust and Clearing Corporation (DTCC). Together, the companies and their affiliates clear and settle virtually all securities transactions in the US market, while the DTC remains the world's largest securities depository.

In contrast to the US, the securities settlement and depository infrastructure in the EU is still quite fragmented. However, some attempt at consolidation is currently underway. At the national level, the integration of CSDs and settlement houses is at a relatively advanced integration stage. Currently, the emphasis is on the cross-border integration of clearing and settlement functions.

The fragmentation of the EU clearing and settlement infrastructure also differs across the main securities markets. In the debt markets, two ICSDs – Euroclear Bank and Clearstream International – already play a dominant role. The ICSDs were originally established to carry out settlement services for the eurobond market. Currently, these two ICSDs provide settlement processing for most types of fixed income trades and to a lesser extent equity transactions. However, in equity markets, settlement is processed in a plethora of national systems involving varying technical requirements, market practices, fiscal procedures and legal environments. Consequently, the cross-border clearing and settlement of equities is more problematic than in bond markets.

However, a recent example of cross-border consolidation of clearing and settlement services is evidenced by the merger of Deutsche Börse Clearing and Cedelbank Luxembourg to form Clearstream International. This merger led to the vertical integration of the trading, clearing and settlement services of the Deutsche Börse. Other initiatives involve ongoing attempts to integrate each Euronext member's settlement system under the Euroclear Group. The announced merger plans between Euroclear and CrestCo UK exemplify horizontal consolidation between domestic trading, clearing, and settlement systems for different securities, that is, fixed income and equities, or cross-border consolidation between two or more national systems for the same kind of instrument.

Will the Consolidation Process of the Clearing and Settlement System Create Natural Monopolies?

The positive effects of consolidation of the clearing and settlement process

The tendency towards a fully consolidated infrastructure is driven by positive externalities, economies of scale, economies of scope and the need for common standards. This also holds true for clearing and settlement agencies. Network externalities allow for the value of services and products offered on the network to rise exponentially with the number of users. Thus, an increase in the number of participants in the clearing and/or settlement system will also increase the range and level of services provided to existing members.

The existence of high fixed investment costs resulting in economies of scale makes a single infrastructure for clearing and settlement more efficient than several systems serving the same market.

The economies of scope, deriving from the need to provide trading, clearing and settlement services in a sequential way, can be fully exploited in the case of the vertical integration of the various infrastructures used in the value chain of a securities transaction.

Finally, by ensuring the adoption of a single standard, the existence of a single integrated infrastructure eliminates the costs and risks associated with the need for users to access several networks with different and incompatible standards.

The negative effects of the consolidation of the clearing and settlement process

Fully consolidated networks also present certain negative externalities. First, a high degree of consolidation implies that the failure of the network has high systematic and contagion risks and costs. Failure of one part of the network could lead to failure of other parts of the integrated network, resulting in contagion. Robustness or system integrity is therefore critical to the safety and soundness of networks.

Second, in a monopoly situation, the lack of competition does not per se provide adequate incentives to the providers to innovate and enhance their product or service, once fixed investment costs have been borne. This can, in turn, determine excessive prices for the users or unjustified barriers to entry for new potential providers.

In the above discussion, it is clear that the positive factors of consolidation in the clearing and settlement system far outweigh the negative factors. Moreover, since the 1990s, competition has crept into many network industries and many public institutions have been transformed into corporations and eventually privatized. Besides, recent developments suggest that network externalities and economies of scale do not necessarily imply a monopoly. In fact, advances in technology may increase the contestability of the market by facilitating the entry of new service providers. However, since the fixed cost of setting up new clearing and settlement systems is very high, unless each new entrant has a minimum number of clients who use the system, the operational efficiency cannot be sustained.

We can conclude that although an integrated clearing and settlement system is not a monopoly and there can be many such integrated clearing and settlement systems, there are, however, certain natural barriers to entry.

What are the Barriers to Consolidation of European Clearing Systems?

Prior to 1999, consolidation in the European trading, clearing and settlement was unthinkable mainly due to the many different currencies in use across the various countries. In May 1999, the common currency, the euro, was adopted across the continent. It was hoped that the capital market would witness a consolidation in trading, clearing, settlements and depository functions. However, the performance so far has been quite dismal. Except for the Euronext exchange and the OMX most trading has remained concentrated in the national stock exchanges of each country. While the Euronext has unified four countries, France, Holland, Belgium and Portugal, the OMX has unified the stock exchanges of Copenhagen, Stockholm, Helsinki, Tallinn, Riga, Vilnius (Lithuania), Oslo and Iceland.

Euronext's clearing system, Clearing 21, merged with LSE's clearing system, London Clearing House (LCH) to form LCH.Clearnet. Trading of both the exchanges, that is, Euronext and LSE, takes place on their respective electronic trading systems – NSC for trading cash products, LIFFE CONNECT for derivatives product in Euronext and SEQUENCE in the LSE. So far LCH.Clearnet is the only consolidated clearing system in Europe.

In Europe, most exchanges have a vertically integrated exchange where the exchange concerned performs the trading, clearing and settlement functions. The German exchange Deutsche Börse, for example, is a vertically integrated exchange. The Deutsche Börse has its trading platform Xetra, the clearing function is performed by Eurex Clearing AG and the settlement delivery function is performed by Clearstream. Clearstream, strangely, has emerged as the international specialized depository operator.

SWX, the Swiss stock exchange, along with Tradepoint, a British ATS, developed the European "blue chips" market. This "blue chips" market trades on the Virt'x framework. Under this clients may choose the settlement delivery system. This model can be perfectly adapted both to an oligopolistic competition and the horizontal concentration process where one operator or only a limited number of operators appear on the clearing or settlement delivery shares.

The ideal scenario is the one where all three systems – trading system, clearing agency and the settling agency – are three separate entities. The scenario is illustrated below.

Trading system

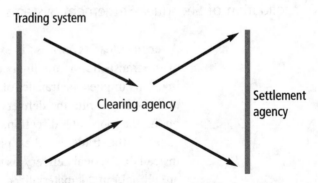

Clearing agency

Settlement agency

The trading system in London is similar to the ideal scenario. Every entity in the processing chain represents an independent functional block. The relationships between the stock exchange (the LSE), the clearing house (LCH.Clearnet) and the central depository (Euroclear) are quite separate.

Although the ideal situation is one in which all three entities are separate, most exchanges in Europe are vertically integrated and do not want to separate the clearing and settlement functions from the exchange functions of trading. This is the main stumbling block in the creation of a consolidated clearing agency in Europe. LCH.Clearnet is, however, a big step and in the future a scenario can be envisaged wherein either the other smaller and independent clearing agencies merge with LCH.Clearnet or merge among themselves to rival LCH.Clearnet. Just as we are hopeful of a consolidation of the European trading platform into one or two major exchanges, similarly we feel that the clearing agencies will also consolidate among themselves to form one or two major clearing agencies to service the entire region. Although presently there appear to be no physical barriers to the consolidation process, the psychological barriers for the creation of a consolidated clearing agency can be broken only with further evolution and a change in mindset.

Consolidation of Securities Settlement Systems

After the clearing process is executed, the settlement of the transaction is the final stage of securities trading. This implies the transfer of money from the buyer to the seller, while the delivery of the securities goes on in the opposite direction. Under most circumstances, the transfer takes place via book entries instead of physical delivery, as the securities in the EU are all held in "dematerialized form". The delivery is executed in a CSD or an ICSD. A CSD is an institution that provides the settlement of domestic trades. An ICSD settles trades in international and internationally traded domestic securities. There are two European ICSDs – Clearstream and Euroclear. While Euroclear settles the transactions on the Euronext, thus acting as the CSD for Belgium, France, Portugal and Holland and also for the LSE, Clearstream acts as the CSD for Germany and Luxembourg.

Banks, as custodians, combined with CSDs or ICSDs are the operators of the securities settlement systems (SSSs). Securities settlement services combine banking services offered by custodian banks (intermediary custody) and central securities settlement services provided by the CSDs.

In addition to the settlement of trades by "outside" parties, trades can be settled internally by local agent banks. These are banks that act on behalf of the investors who engage in trading. When a trade takes place between investors who happen to use the same local agent bank, the latter can settle "on his own books", without needing a CSD or an ICSD. Hence, although in a single country or even a group of countries, one often finds one ICSD, several players are active in the process of settling securities trades.

A third type of institution is present in the European clearing, settlement and safekeeping industry. They are the "custodians" whose function is the custody and safekeeping of the securities. Safekeeping entails more than merely keeping a record of the existing positions, since assets need to be serviced. It is possible to segregate the safekeeping and the asset servicing activity from the settlement services. On the one hand, all the securities that are emitted in a country are deposited in a single CSD and on the other hand, all the investors have their securities account with a single monopoly local agent bank. It is possible for the local agent bank to settle all transactions in any particular security, since every trade merely requires the debiting and crediting of securities and cash accounts that are all held with the local agent bank. When the companies decide on their dividend policy, the CSD becomes active and transmits to the single monopoly local agent bank all the necessary funds against the required coupons.

SSSs operated by the CSDs are the final stage of the securities chain. After being traded on the market trading systems (stock exchanges, over-the-counter markets, ATSs) and often cleared in the clearing houses, all transactions have to be settled in an SSS. SSSs are institutional arrangements necessary to finalize securities transactions. Through the SSS it administers, the CSD provides the settlement service infrastructure for banks which use their services for their customers to achieve a securities settlement instruction, an investor needs a bank acting as a custodian and a CSD which operates the SSS (settlement function). This arrangement is quite simple for domestic operations: banks (custodians) are members of the national CSD which operates a national SSS to settle their trades. For cross-border operations, securities settlement is more complex since there is no such institutional and structured arrangement.

A fully integrated settlement and custodial service provider is preferable to the use of the intermediate local agent since the agents have to be paid for their services. This increases the cost of the settlement functions to the investors.

The Relationships Between Sub-custodians and CSDs

Within the money payment system, the banks manage the deposit accounts of economic agents and they ensure, on their authority, the payment service for their account. A payment initiated by X for Y supposes an interbank settlement to be effective in central money by the registration in the central accounts opened by bank A and bank B in the books of the central bank.

Similarly, in the securities transaction too the same hierarchical and centralized organization may occur: the custodians manage the securities accounts of agents X and Y and ensure the securities "transport service" from one to the other. The securities deposited by X to A are "redeposited" to the central depository that ensures the custody of all securities issued on the "assets territory". Therefore, the custodians are only the intermediate depositories of the securities they "have on custody" for the account of their clients.

However, as compared to money, securities operate on a different logic: while X has securities, it is the owner and can enjoy the features of ownership – interest for interest bearing financial products and dividends for share certificates. Also the local custodian is only the depository of the securities. It does not own the securities and it cannot lend them to other economic agents.

The Role of Global Custodians in the Cross-border Trades

Global custodians process securities in an administrative manner within an environment of different jurisdictions, more often by subcontracting to local sub-custodians. In some countries, the ICSDs are not permitted to have direct access to the CSDs. Consequently, ICSDs may not have accounts with every CSD. In such cases, the ICSDs have to deal with local correspondents like sub-custodians. The securities are immobilized with the local sub-custodians on behalf of the ICSDs. The sub-custodian banks have direct access to a CSD of the country in which they are located and to the settlement delivery systems managed by this CSD.

Increasingly, cross-border trades significantly increase the role of the global custodians. This will result in consolidation of business among the custodians. Local CSDs may develop a link between themselves or ICSDs may also buy local CSDs. By merging with local CSDs, ICSDs could monopolize all the securities flow and thus position themselves as international custodians.

In Europe a consolidated global custodian is difficult to implement due to fragmentation in every sphere of trading. Trading systems vary from country to country, there are no proper linkages between the different countries and the rules and practices are also heterogeneous. Consequently, the operations require multiple human interventions and thus the operations are less reliable (problems of data reentering/operational risk), longer and more expensive. Under these circumstances, the STP procedures are impossible to implement at the moment at the international level. However, regulation and proper implementation could change the scenario and subsequently enable the implementation of a collective control for the development of a global custodian in Europe.

In the long run, the European custodians Euroclear and Clearstream may merge to create a common custodian to cater for the European market.

What Prevents the Consolidation Process of SSSs in Europe?

The fragmentation of the European securities settlement infrastructure is one barrier which prevents the integration of the European financial markets. The two Giovanni (2001, 2003) reports on the problems raised by cross-border clearing and settlement throughout Europe have pointed out 15 fiscal, legal and technical barriers which have to be removed. The lack of integration between SSSs throughout Europe is one of the technical barriers which prevent the financial integration of capital markets aimed for by the Financial Services Action Plan. With the new Investment Services Directive and a Directive on securities settlement, the improvement of cross-border operations in a more integrated market is necessary to facilitate securities circulation, especially in the Eurozone. Free choice of localization of securities settlement and custody should be possible. Competition and consolidation in the custodian market leads to rationalization of the securities settlement procedures.

Cross-border settlements in Europe have to be simplified. A consolidation process is currently on its way between national SSSs, especially for exchanges which have merged, for example the ESES RGV project in the Euronext Group. ESES RGV will become the single settlement facility for all Euronext's markets by 2007. The ICSDs – Euroclear and Clearstream – intend to deliver cross-border settlement services in Europe through the Single Access Plate-form project led by Euroclear. They compete directly with global custodians which provide central securities settlement services through their sub-custodian networks. The complexity of the consolidation process in the securities settlement industry is linked to the characteristic of this market. The custody and securities settlement market is composed of two kinds of complementary infrastructures: CSDs provide central infrastructures through the SSS which allows the circulation of securities' transfers and securities' bookkeeping for their clients (secondary SSS or securities' settlement facilities). CSDs manage central market infrastructures and custodians manage customer-oriented facilities (custody and securities transfer for investors). This separation is nebulous in Europe: ICSDs indeed play these two roles. They operate SSSs and they also have banking functions.

A domestic security settlement service requires two complementary firms – an intermediary custodian (IC) and an ultimate custodian (UC). An IC is usually a bank in charge of settlement and custody services for investors and a UC is a CSD which administers the central SSS. An IC holds the securities account in the books of the CSD (UC) which operates the SSS for securities transfer between custodians. A CSD is a monopolistic producer of the component settlement (it operates a single national SSS). There are several banks which provide the intermediary custody activity. For cross-border operations, the organization is more complex. Custodians have to manage this organizational complexity due to the absence or inadequacy of direct links between CSDs and ICSDs. Currently, domestic securities never leave the country issuing the security: they have to be centrally held in the books of the national CSD. SSSs cannot be substituted as long as some restrictions remain: location of settlement, barriers of remote access and restrictions on localization of securities. These barriers have to be removed to improve cross-border operations.

Can Economies of Scale be Achieved with the Consolidation of the SSSs?

There is considerable potential for cost savings from expanding jointly the depository and settlement businesses across regions. The centralized US system is found to be the most cost-effective settlement system. The latest step in the consolidation process in the US has been the integration of the operations of the DTC and the NSCC under a common holding company, the DTCC. Together, the companies and their affiliates clear and settle virtually all securities transactions in the US market, while the DTC remains the world's largest securities depository.

In contrast to the US, the securities settlement and depository infrastructure in the EU is still quite fragmented, although some efforts towards a more integrated infrastructure are underway. At the national level, the integration of CSDs and settlement houses is at a relatively advanced stage, so that the emphasis is now on the need for reforms in the cross-border settlement of securities.

The fragmentation of the EU clearing and settlement infrastructure also differs across the main securities markets. For example, in the debt markets, two ICSDs, Euroclear Bank and Clearstream International, already play a dominant role. The ICSDs were originally established to carry out settlement services for the eurobond market. Currently, they provide settlement processing for most types of fixed income trades and to a lesser extent to the equity transactions. However, in equity markets, settlement is processed in a plethora of national systems involving varying technical requirements, market practices, fiscal procedures and legal environments. Consequently, the cross-border clearing and settlement of equities is more problematic than in bond markets.

However, some attempts point towards cross-border consolidation in the European clearing and settlement industry, as evidenced by the recent merger of Deutsche Börse Clearing and Cedelbank Luxembourg to form Clearstream International. Here the purpose was to achieve vertical integration by linking trading, clearing and settlement services in a single institution. Other initiatives involve ongoing attempts to integrate each Euronext member's settlement system under the Euroclear Group. The merger between Euroclear and CrestCo UK exemplifies horizontal consolidation between domestic trading, clearing and settlement systems for different securities, that is, fixed income and equities.

The US consolidated system acts as the benchmark for the most cost-effective settlement system. In Europe and the Asia-Pacific region, individually the exchanges are cost-efficient with small businesses. The moment volumes increase, costs also increase. The operating costs of carrying cross-border settlement are much higher than operating a domestic CSD, reflecting the current complexities of EU international securities settlement and differences in the underlying scope of ICSD services. Operating costs will, however, decrease over time as more investment is put into implementing new systems for upgrading the technology.

In the long run, expansions and the pooling of depository and settlement businesses will enhance savings in unit costs for small and medium-sized institutions. This effect is less pronounced for bigger service providers. Smaller institutions should therefore accelerate investment plans, reduce prices, form implicit mergers, and thereby achieve higher production at a lower unit cost in their depository and settlement businesses.

A well-regulated system also plays an important role in the creation of a consolidated settlement system. However, a consolidation of settlement systems in the EU is quite unfeasible due to the plethora of integration barriers. Changes in the regulatory framework could prove to be beneficial and collaborations among the existing CSDs in the EU may be feasible in the long run.

The Future of Stock Exchanges

With technology affecting all arenas of stock exchanges, the future of the exchange is quite different from what it is today. Of course trading in stocks and other financial products will continue for years to come. But technology has revolutionized the concept of trading and may gradually eliminate intermediaries like the broker-traders. Already the concept of the stock market as a location to trade in shares and other financial products has vanished. Internet-based trading and trading on the alternative trading systems will gradually evolve as the norm.

Technology will further enable quantitative decision making and there will be much greater volumes of trading. But with the ATSs and internet-based trading growing, existing exchanges will face a cut in trading and listing fees. This will result in a squeezing of revenues for the exchanges which will in turn make it unviable for the exchanges to remain predominantly local or national exchanges. With revenues falling, most exchanges will demutualize themselves and the industry will witness a major consolidation and integration among the exchanges.

Changes in the regulatory framework will increase cross-border trading. This will further promote cross-border integration among the exchanges. Further improvements in technology will lead to the emergence of a handful of exchanges trading in all segments of financial products, with clients spread globally but regulated by one standard set of norms and trades settled in one ICSD in the STP technology.

Although it may be difficult to visualize such a scenario today, this is not an unrealistic projection.

CHAPTER 4

Regulation and Investor Protection

The evolution of financial markets has been particularly significant in the past few decades with regard to intermediaries, capital markets and financial instruments. Structural changes have mainly involved the more traditional financial operators in banking, but have also involved investment firms and insurance companies.

With the advent of the new millennium and the legacy of globalization there is bound to be a lot of changes in the financial markets too. In an increasingly global market, the ensuing trend has been for a greater harmonization of global stock exchanges. Globalization has had a knock-on effect, with one market implementing new regulations and technological advances.

Not all stock markets are the same, nor is any one stock market appropriate for all types of companies. Markets vary by listing requirements and maintenance standards as well as by their rules and regulations governing trade execution, reporting and settlement. Markets also vary according to market structure and trading mechanisms.

Regulatory arrangements have also been the object of significant change. Such dynamics are at the center of attention at international venues. A number of countries (the US, the UK, Australia and Japan) are in fact presently radically changing their regulatory systems.

The theoretical underpinning for public intervention in economic matters is traditionally based on the need to correct market imperfections and the unfair distribution of resources. The regulation of the financial system can be viewed as a particularly important case of public control over the economy. The accumulation of capital and the allocation of financial resources constitute an essential aspect in the process of the economic development of a nation. The peculiarities of financial intermediation and the operators who perform this function justify the existence of a broader system of controls with respect to other forms of economic activity. Various theoretical motivations have been advanced to support the opportunity of particularly stringent regulations for banks and other financial intermediaries. Such motivations are based on the existence of particular forms of market failure in the credit and financial sectors.

The Objectives of Financial Market Regulations

A primary objective of financial market regulation is the pursuit of macroeconomic and microeconomic stability. Safeguarding the stability of the system translates into macro-controls over the financial exchanges, clearing houses and securities settlement systems. Measures pertaining to the micro-stability of intermediaries can be divided into two categories: general rules on the stability of all business enterprises and entrepreneurial activities, such as the legally required amount of capital, borrowing limits and integrity requirements; and more specific rules due to the special nature of financial intermediation, such as

risk-based capital ratios, limits to portfolio investments and the regulation of off-balance activities.

The second objective of financial regulation is transparency in the market and in intermediaries and investor
protection. This is linked to the more general objective
of equity in the distribution of available resources and
may be mapped into the search for equity in the distribution of information as a precious good among operators. At the macro-level, transparency rules impose
equal treatment (for example, rules regarding takeovers
and public offers) and the correct dissemination of
information (insider trading, manipulation and the rules
dealing with exchanges' microstructure and price
discovery mechanisms). At the micro-level, such rules
aim at non-discrimination in relationships among intermediaries and different customers.

A third objective of financial market regulation, linked
with the general objective of efficiency, is the safeguard and promotion of competition in the financial
intermediation sector. This requires rules for control
over the structure of competition in the markets and, at
the micro-level, regulations in the matter of concentra-
tions, cartels and abuse of dominant positions.

Self-regulation

Stock exchanges have evolved as a trading place
where broker-traders congregate to "speculate" either
directly or on behalf of other "customers". Such speculation has always remained a double-edged sword.
While on the one hand, speculation could lead to
bumper gains, so also it could lead to a total stock
market crash. It is due to these failures that stock
exchange transactions have become embedded in a

regulatory framework which distinguishes them from unregulated market arenas. One of the most distinct traits of stock exchange regulation traditionally has been its private, self-regulatory character. The American and British systems have long been prototypical examples of this model of self-regulation. Originating in the 1790s, the NYSE and the LSE developed essentially as cartels of stockholders or investment houses, banded together by price fixing. The stock exchanges of yore have remained as exclusive clubs with restricted membership while internally they maintained control over their members. This control was "self-regulation".

The institutionalization of stock exchanges was closely linked with the incorporation of the merchant class. Organized markets were mostly implemented by local chambers of commerce and enjoyed the status of public law bodies. Trading was governed by rules that were embedded within the professional ethics of the merchant business. Internally the exchanges were governed by a number of self-regulatory bodies which dealt among other things with admission to security listings, fees for equity trading or disciplinary procedures when exchange rules were breached.

As long as the regulatory parties as well as the regulated parties remained confined within the same jurisdiction or rather the same stock exchange, self-regulatory bodies were competent to handle any breach of rules. As the stock exchange market expanded to other regions or across different stock exchanges, self-regulation became difficult as each exchange followed different regulations. This is when the differences in regulations led to discrepancies and consequently, it was necessary to have government intervention.

Is Government Regulation Necessary?

Self-regulation in the stock exchanges has existed since time immemorial. In the absence of government regulation, corporations were still compelled to disclose information about their financial affairs. They did this partly because of economic incentives and partly because private stock exchanges imposed rules on members. For example, prior to the securities acts, all companies listed on the New York and American Stock Exchanges were required by the two exchanges to make their financial statements available to the public. Also, over 90 percent of all companies traded on the NYSE in 1933 were audited by independent certified public accountants. The legislation requiring periodic financial reporting and the audits of that information was passed in 1934.

Similarly, the UK securities market continues to rely on a corporate disclosure system that is privately run. Although the UK has laws that govern disclosure by companies, most of the functions performed by the SEC in the USA are performed by the LSE, which is not an agency of the government. Unlike American securities regulation, British laws are self-contained and allow very limited discretionary power for government administrators. The result is a system that is not only less cumbersome, less costly and more flexible, but also has fewer frauds. Clearly, self-regulation is also effective and can exist in the economy.

Moreover, it has been observed a number of times that government regulations may hinder the functioning of companies. Frequently government regulators have attempted to assert greater control on the private sector, not for reasons of good corporate governance but rather to thrust policy makers' ideas on the system.

Regulatory Framework

We cannot easily define which type of regulatory framework is suited for the regulation and supervision of financial markets. Loosely, we can identify four approaches for regulation of the financial markets. They are:

- Institutional supervision
- Supervision by objectives
- Functional supervision
- Single regulator supervision.

Institutional Supervision

In the more traditional institutional approach, supervision is performed over each single category of financial operator over each single segment of the financial market and is assigned to a distinct agency for the entire complex of activities. In this regulatory model we have three supervisory authorities acting as watchdogs over the three segments of the financial markets, namely banks, financial intermediaries and mutual funds and insurance companies. The authorities control intermediaries and markets through entry selection processes (for example, authorizations and enrolling procedures in special registers), constant monitoring of the business activities (controls, inspections and sanctions) and eventual exits from the market (suspensions or removals).

Institutional regulation facilitates the effective realization of control, being performed with regard to subjects that are regulated as to every aspect of their activity and as to all the objectives of regulation. Each intermediary and market has only one supervisory authority as a counterpart. The latter's function becomes a highly specialized area and, as a result, duplication of controls is avoided and the cost of regulation can be considerably reduced.

However, since this type of regulation entails the specialization of intermediaries, it creates a building up of large financial conglomerates. In the context of the fast erosion of boundaries separating the various institutions, it is no longer possible to establish whether a particular subject is a bank, a non-banking intermediary or an insurance company; or whether a group is involved more in one or other of such activities. There is a risk that "parallel" systems of intermediation are created, reflecting the diversity of the respective control authorities. Thus, the way the controls are set up may become a destabilizing factor rather than a stabilizing factor. Moreover, the intermediaries may be induced to choose their judicial status in a way which is contingent on the different rules that discipline different status.

Another disadvantage of this system is that when a single authority supervises a category of subjects and pursues more than one objective, the results of the control activity might not be effective in the event that different objectives are in conflict.

Supervision by Objectives

The supervisory model by objectives postulates that all intermediaries and markets be subjected to the control of more than one authority, each single authority being responsible for one objective of regulation, regardless of both the legal form of the intermediaries and the functions or activities they perform. Under this system, an authority is to watch over both market stability and the solvency of each intermediary, whether in banking, finance or insurance; another authority will be responsible for the transparency of financial markets and will control the behavior of banks, financial intermediaries and insurance companies towards customers; a third authority will guarantee and safeguard competition over the entire financial market and among intermediaries.

This regulatory model is effective in a highly integrated market, where numerous operators are working in a variety of different business sectors but at the same time excessive controls are not required by any of them.

The most attractive feature of this scheme is that it provides uniform regulation for the different subjects engaged in the same activities.

However, each intermediary is subject to the control of more than one authority, which makes the system a very expensive one. The intermediaries may have to justify the same action to a whole set of authorities for different reasons, and, vice versa, a deficit of controls may occur whenever the exact areas of responsibility are not clearly identifiable in specific cases.

Functional Supervision

In the functional supervision model, or supervision "by activity", each type of financial service should be regulated by a given authority independently of the operator who offers it. This approach has the important advantage that it calls for the same rules to be applied to intermediaries who perform the same activity of financial intermediation even though such operators may fall into different categories from a legal standpoint. This approach fosters economies of specialization within the supervisory authorities and might represent a rather attractive solution for the regulation of integrated, advanced financial markets. However, this model has one major flaw: there is the risk of an excessive division of competencies among the regulatory agencies.

A further disadvantage of the functional approach is that finally what is subject to failure is not the activity performed, but the institution. If serious problems of stability occurred, it would be essential to guarantee protection and oversight with regard to the institutions rather than individual operations.

Single Regulator Supervision

The single regulator supervisory model is based on just one control authority, separated from the central bank, with responsibility over all markets and intermediaries regardless of whether in the banking, financial or insurance sector. This authority would be concerned with all the objectives of regulation – stability, transparency and investor protection.

In regulatory practice, the centralized supervisory model has typically characterized the early stages of financial system development, often in periods when the central bank was the only institution that supervised the activity of financial intermediaries. In recent times, due to globalization and the integration of markets, the British government brought this model back with the creation of the Financial Services Authority (FSA).

The advantages of this approach lie in the economies of scale that it produces. Fixed costs and logistical expenses, the costs of administrative personnel and compensation for top management are all considerably reduced. Moreover, this scheme calls for a unified view which is particularly useful and effective with respect to multifunctional groups and conglomerates. Moreover, it reduces the costs of supervision.

However, the validity of this model depends on the internal organization of the regulatory body. If the numerous areas of competence and specialization are not well structured and coordinated, the risk is to slow the decision-making process. Also, the presence of a sole regulator might render collusive relations more immediate and direct. Finally, it might aggravate problems of self-contradiction in the event that the authority should find itself forced to pursue conflicting supervisory objectives. This sort of problem may in part be overcome thanks to an internal organization divided "by objectives", but the fact that there is only one top management would end up in the prevalence of a single objective as a final consequence of the decision-making process.

Which Supervision Model is the Optimal Model?

Although it is difficult to arrive at a conclusion of the optimal model of supervision, the single regulator model is generally considered as the most appropriate model. It not only reduces duplicity of functions but also clearly reduces the cost of supervision. Moreover, when the markets become integrated across regions, a single supervisor eliminates confusion and thereby increases efficiency in the market. The only reason why there is difficulty in integrating the EU market has been due to the different regulators functioning in the different countries. Meanwhile, the different exchanges in the USA have easily integrated because the SEC is the sole regulating authority in the region. However, there are a few self-regulated exchanges – the NYSE and the NASD, which operates the NASDAQ system.

The primary mission of the Securities Exchange Commission (SEC) is to protect investors and maintain the integrity of the securities markets. The SEC requires public companies to disclose meaningful financial and other information to the public. The SEC also oversees other key participants in the securities world, including stock exchanges, broker-dealers, investment advisers, mutual funds, and public utility holding companies. The SEC is concerned primarily with promoting the disclosure of important information, enforcing the securities laws, and protecting investors who interact with these various organizations and individuals. Although it is the primary overseer and regulator of the US securities markets, the SEC works closely with many other institutions, including Congress, other federal departments and agencies, the self-regulatory organizations (for example, the stock exchanges), state securities regulators, and various private sector organizations.

In the UK, the FSA is an independent non-governmental body, given statutory powers by the Financial Services and Markets Act 2000. The FSA is now the single statutory regulator responsible for regulating deposit taking, insurance and investment business. The FSA is also responsible for tackling market abuse, promoting public understanding of the financial system and reducing financial crime.

Euronext is the first attempt at integrating the European markets, with the exchange providing trading facilities to five different countries – Belgium, France, the Netherlands and Portugal as well as the UK (derivatives only). However, for regulatory reasons, notably regarding the admission of securities to listing and tender offers, as well as to respect each member market's domestic environment, the five market operators – now wholly owned subsidiaries of Euronext N.V. – continue to exist separately.

Do Exchanges Prefer to have Regulatory Power?

Exchanges prefer to regulate their market independently from government authority

In a survey conducted by the World Federation of Exchanges (WFE) on market regulations by exchanges in January 2004, it was proved that most exchanges prefer to regulate their own market. The survey was conducted by Professor Roberta Karmel of Brooklyn University. Most of the exchanges are engaged in market regulation. Virtually all exchanges believe that regulation is a part of their brand and that they should make every effort to maintain their regulatory authority by adapting to changing market conditions and changing laws by the use of technology and creative solutions to the new conflicts of interest which are emerging from new markets and new organizational forms. Many continue to license trading members and supervise clearing and settlement activities. Many continue to regulate listed company disclosures and corporate governance. The survey also concluded that the costs of regulation are a significant portion of exchange operating expenses. Moreover, expenses on regulation are rising over the years.

Regulation in the USA

The "roaring twenties" was a time of exuberance in the USA, and one of the most famous signs of exuberance was the roaring stock market. But underneath all the giddiness was a dark undercurrent of questionable practices that ultimately worsened the effects of the stock market crash of 1929. Publicly traded companies were not required to report financial results to the public, there was no prohibition against insider trading and other forms of market manipulation, and there was no central body to enforce the law which did exist. Because of this lack of regulation, the extent of the crash and the subsequent Depression took many people by surprise.

The stock market carnage spilled into the US banking industry where banks lost heavily on proprietary stock investments. Fearing that banks would be unable to repay money in their accounts, depositors staged a "run" on banks. Thousands of US banks collapsed. The US Congress passed legislation designed to prevent abuses of the securities market and restore investors' confidence.

Securities Act of 1933

Often referred to as the "truth in securities" law, the Securities Act of 1933 has two basic objectives. It:

- Requires that investors receive financial and other significant information concerning securities being offered for public sale
- Prohibits deceit, misrepresentations, and other fraud in the sale of securities.

Purpose of Registration

A primary means of accomplishing these goals is the disclosure of important financial information through the registration of securities. This information enables investors, not the government, to make informed judgments about whether to purchase a company's securities. While the SEC requires that the information provided be accurate, it does not guarantee it. Investors who purchase securities and suffer losses have important recovery rights if they can prove that there was incomplete or inaccurate disclosure of important information.

The Registration Process

In general, securities sold in the US must be registered. The registration forms that companies file should provide essential facts while minimizing the burden and expense of complying with the law. In general, registration forms call for:

- A description of the company's properties and business

- A description of the security to be offered for sale

- Information about the management of the company

- Certification of financial statements by independent accountants.

Registration statements and prospectuses become public shortly after filing with the SEC. Once the US domestic companies file their financial statements, they are available on the EDGAR database. Registration statements are subject to scrutiny for compliance with disclosure requirements.

However, not all offerings of securities have to be registered with the SEC. Some exemptions from the registration requirement include:

- Private offerings to a limited number of persons or institutions

- Offerings of limited size
- Intrastate offerings
- Securities of municipal, state, and federal governments.

By exempting many small offerings from the registration process, the SEC seeks to foster capital formation by lowering the cost of offering securities to the public.

The SEC has five commissioners, appointed by the president for five-year terms, one of which expires each year. No more than three of the commissioners can be members of the same political party. The four main divisions are: the Division of Corporate Finance, the Division of Market Regulation, the Division of Investment Management, and the Division of Enforcement.

The Division of Corporate Finance

The main function of this division is to make sure that all publicly traded companies disclose all the information they are supposed to, both financial and otherwise. The quarterly report that companies have to file with the SEC is called a 10-Q, and the annual report is called a 10-K. Both reports contain financial statements as well as information about the company's operations, competitive environment, unusual expenses or charges, and more. The Division of Corporate Finance also reviews applications for IPOs (called prospectuses, or S-1 filings) and documents relating to mergers and acquisitions.

The Division of Market Regulation

This division oversees the participants in the secondary securities markets, primarily broker-dealers (represented by the NASD) and the stock markets themselves. These organizations make and enforce many of their own rules, and in fact they are officially known under the federal securities laws as self-regulatory organizations (SROs). The SEC has to approve these rules and make sure they conform to the various federal securities laws, and it also hears appeals from the regulatory divisions of the various SROs. The main purpose of this division is to make sure that the markets are operating fairly and smoothly, without practices such as insider trading.

The Division of Market Regulation also oversees the Securities Investor Protection Corporation (SIPC). The SIPC is a non-profit insurance company that is similar to the banking industry's FDIC. While the SIPC does not protect investors against losses due to trading or company fraud, it does ensure that investors retain ownership of their shares should their brokers go under.

The Division of Investment Management

This division is responsible for regulating the practices of mutual funds and investment advisers. It makes sure that funds and advisers are properly registered and keeps an eye on their sales and advertising techniques, all of which are regulated by the Investment Company Act of 1940 and other laws. It ensures that funds and fund companies issue proxy statements and stockholder reports, among other documents. The Division of Investment Management also oversees public utilities such as power and gas companies, which were once cesspools of rampant abuse before being put under control of the SEC in 1935.

The Division of Enforcement

This division is the policing arm of the SEC, responsible for enforcing all the various securities laws and investigating violations. It only became a separate division in 1972 (before that, the other divisions enforced their own laws), but today it's probably the most active division of the SEC. The explosion in popularity of the internet has resulted in a proliferation of internet-based investment scams, which the Division of Enforcement has made a concerted effort to control. One of the scams involves illegal "touting" of small-cap stocks on the internet. Touting a stock means promoting it, often with outlandish claims for its future potential, without revealing that you are being paid to do so by the company.

In addition to these four divisions, there are two offices of the SEC that serve important functions. The Office of the General Counsel is the legal arm of the SEC, representing it in court cases and providing general legal advice. The Office of Compliance, Inspections and Examinations makes sure that stock exchanges, brokers, and investment advisers are complying with securities laws by conducting regular examinations and inspections. It's a sort of middleman between the first three divisions described above (which make the rules) and the Division of Enforcement (which enforces them). All the various parts of the SEC work together to try to make the US securities markets operate as fairly and openly as possible.

Securities Exchange Act of 1934

With this Act, Congress created the Securities and Exchange Commission. The Act gives the SEC broad authority over all aspects of the securities industry. This includes the power to register, regulate, and oversee brokerage firms, transfer agents, and clearing agencies as well as the nation's securities SROs. The various stock exchanges, such as the NYSE, and American Stock Exchange are SROs. The National Association of Securities Dealers, which operates the NASDAQ system, is also an SRO.

The Act also identifies and prohibits certain types of conduct in the markets and provides the SEC with disciplinary powers over regulated entities and persons associated with them. The Act also empowers the SEC to require periodic reporting of information by companies with publicly traded securities.

Corporate Reporting

Companies with more than $10 million in assets, whose securities are held by more than 500 stockholders, must file annual and other periodic reports. These reports are available to the public through the SEC's EDGAR database.

Proxy Solicitations

The Securities Exchange Act also governs the disclosure of materials used to solicit stockholders' votes in annual or special meetings held for the election of directors and the approval of other corporate action. This information, contained in proxy materials, must be filed with the SEC in advance of any solicitation to ensure compliance with the disclosure rules. Solicitations, whether by management or stockholder groups, must disclose all important facts concerning the issues on which stockholders are asked to vote.

Tender Offers

The Securities Exchange Act requires disclosure of important information by anyone seeking to acquire more than 5 percent of a company's securities by direct purchase or tender offer. Such an offer is often extended in an effort to gain control of the company. As with the proxy rules, this allows stockholders to make informed decisions on these critical corporate events.

Insider Trading

The securities laws broadly prohibit fraudulent activities of any kind in connection with the offer, purchase, or sale of securities. These provisions are the basis for many types of disciplinary actions, including actions against fraudulent insider trading. Insider trading is illegal when a person trades a security while in possession of material non-public information in violation of a duty to withhold the information or refrain from trading.

Registration of Exchanges, Associations, and Others

The Act requires a variety of market participants to register with the SEC, including exchanges, brokers and dealers, transfer agents, and clearing agencies. Registration with these organizations involves filing disclosure documents that are updated on a regular basis.

The exchanges and the NASD are identified as SROs. SROs must create rules that allow for disciplining members for improper conduct and for establishing measures to ensure market integrity and investor protection. SRO-proposed rules are published for comment before final SEC review and approval.

Public Utility Holding Company Act of 1935

Interstate holding companies engaged, through subsidiaries, in the electric utility business or the retail distribution of natural or manufactured gas are subject to regulation under this Act. These companies, unless specifically exempted, are required to submit reports providing detailed information concerning the organization, financial structure, and operations of the holding company and its subsidiaries. Holding companies are subject to SEC regulations on matters such as the structure of their utility systems, transactions among companies that are part of the holding company utility system, acquisitions, business combinations, the issue and sale of securities, and financing transactions.

Trust Indenture Act of 1939

This Act applies to debt securities such as bonds, debentures, and notes that are offered for public sale. Even though such securities may be registered under the Securities Act, they may not be offered for sale to the public unless a formal agreement between the issuer of bonds and the bondholder, known as the trust indenture, conforms to the standards of this Act.

Investment Company Act of 1940

This Act regulates the organization of companies, including mutual funds, that engage primarily in investing, reinvesting, and trading in securities, and whose own securities are offered to the investing public. The regulation is designed to minimize conflicts of interest that arise in these complex operations. The Act requires these companies to disclose their financial condition and investment policies to investors when stock is initially sold and, subsequently, on a regular basis. The focus of this Act is on disclosure to the investing public of information about the fund and its investment objectives, as well as on investment company structure and operations. It is important to remember that the Act does not permit the SEC to directly supervise the investment decisions or activities of these companies or judge the merits of their investments.

Investment Advisers Act of 1940

This law regulates investment advisers. With certain exceptions, this Act requires that firms or sole practitioners compensated for advising others about securities investments must register with the SEC and conform to regulations designed to protect investors. Since the Act was amended in 1996, generally only advisers who have at least $25 million of assets under management or advise a registered investment company must register with the SEC.

Sarbanes-Oxley Act of 2002

On July 30, 2002, President George Bush signed into law the Sarbanes-Oxley (SOX) Act of 2002. The Act mandated a number of reforms to enhance corporate responsibility, enhance financial disclosures and combat corporate and accounting fraud, and created the Public Company Accounting Oversight Board (PCAOB), to oversee the activities of the auditing profession.

Provisions of the Sarbanes-Oxley Act

The main provisions of the Sarbanes-Oxley Act are as follows:

- Certification of financial reports by CEOs and CFOs

- Ban on personal loans to any executive officer and director

- Accelerated reporting of trades by "insiders"

- Prohibition on insider trades during pension fund blackout periods

- Public reporting of CEO and CFO compensation and profits

- Additional disclosure

- Auditor independence, including outright bans on certain types of work and pre-certification by the company's audit committee of all other non-audit work

- Criminal and civil penalties for securities violations

- Significantly longer jail sentences and larger fines for corporate executives who knowingly and willfully misstate financial statements

- Prohibition on audit firms providing extra value-added services to their clients, including actuarial services, legal and extra services (such as consulting) unrelated to their audit work

- A requirement that publicly traded companies furnish independent annual audit reports on the existence and condition (that is, reliability) of internal controls as they relate to financial reporting.

PCAOB's Requirements

Auditing companies have to fulfill certain criteria set by the PCAOB. The criteria that have to be fulfilled are as follows:

- The design of controls over relevant assertions related to all significant accounts and disclosures in the financial statements

- Information about how significant transactions are initiated, authorized, supported, processed, and reported

- Enough information about the flow of transactions to identify where material misstatements due to error or fraud could occur

- Controls designed to prevent or detect fraud, including who performs the controls and the regulated segregation of duties

- Controls over the period-end financial reporting process

- Controls over safeguarding of assets

- The results of management's testing and evaluation.

Internal Controls

The key element of the Act is that it requires a report of the internal controls that a company has in place to ensure compliance with the Act itself. It mandates that CEOs and CFOs of each company must file Internal Control Over Financial Reporting and Certification of Disclosure in Exchange Act Periodic Reports.

This Act requires management to document and assess the effectiveness of their internal controls over financial reporting. SOX 404 Compliance has had serious effects on those found to have material weaknesses in internal control. In this Act, companies must, for the first time, provide attestation of internal control assessment. This presents new challenges to businesses, specifically, documentation of control procedures related to information technology.

Additionally, the PCAOB has also issued guidelines on how management should render their opinion. The main point of these guidelines is that management should use an internal control framework such as COSO (which describes how to assess the control environment, determine control objectives, perform risk assesments, and identify controls and monitor compliance). Companies have almost uniformly elected COSO as the standard when choosing an internal control framework.

IT Controls, IT Audit and the SOX Act

With the IT revolution, most corporate functions are manged electronically. Therefore, it is apparent that IT plays a vital role in internal control. Chief information officers (CIOs) are responsible for the security, accuracy and reliability of the systems that manage and report the financial data. Systems such as enterprise resource planning are deeply integrated in the initiating, authorizing, processing, and reporting of financial data. As such, they are inextricably linked to the overall financial reporting process and need to be assessed, along with other important processes, for compliance with the SOX Act. So, although the Act signals a fundamental change in business operations and financial reporting, and places responsibility for corporate financial reporting on the CEO and CFO, the CIO plays a significant role in the signoff of financial statements.

Compliance with SOX Act Increases the Cost

The SOX Act requires that corporates update their information systems to comply with the control and reporting requirements. Systems which provide document management, access to financial data, or long-term storage of information must provide auditing capabilities. In most cases, this required significant changes to, or even complete replacement of, existing systems which were designed without the needed level of auditing details. This led to steep increases in costs to meet the SOX compliance norms. However, non-compliance comes with an even higher cost in terms of stiffer penalties and jail sentences.

Less visible costs have also been incurred. Although hard to measure, these costs are even larger than the direct costs. Some non-American companies have threatened not to list on the American exchanges due to the higher costs incurred, others have recently delisted due partly to the SOX Act, and some 20 percent of public companies in a study by Foley & Lardner, a law firm, said that they were considering going private to avoid the costs of the Act. However, it would be regrettable if a law intended to improve the quantity and quality of financial information available to investors led many companies to seek relatively unregulated forms of jurisdictions – and right now that does seem to be happening.

Another hidden cost which many business leaders complain of is the effect which the law will have in discouraging risk. Steps to discourage risks of the kind taken by Enron might seem entirely warranted – indeed, you might argue, that was the whole point of the law – but many of the statute's critics say that, in threatening (as they see it) to criminalize ordinary business mistakes, it goes too far. Small firms, put at a particular disadvantage by the added regulatory burden, also tend to be more inclined than big ones to take risks.

Technological Changes and Regulatory Responses of the SEC

In the past decade, financial markets have witnessed widespread technological advances that increased market information and enhanced information flow. These recent advances in ICT result in markets that are more efficient and transparent and better able to handle increased trading volume. Moreover, the benefits of recent technological developments have not been limited to the markets, but have extended to all security industry professionals.

The SEC has undertaken a number of initiatives that relate to the use of technology in the marketplace. The SEC has also tried to be receptive to industry requests for guidance regarding how to administer regulations in the technologically advanced market. The SEC has modified certain rules and interpretations that may inhibit the use of technological innovations.

To increase transparency and improve opportunities for the best execution of customer orders, the SEC adopted the following:

Electronic communication systems and execution rules

■ **Limit Order Display Rule** – This rule requires exchange specialists and over-the-counter market makers to immediately display in their bid or offer both the price and the full size of each customer limit order that will improve their quoted price in a particular security.

■ **Quote Rule** – The SEC amended this rule as per the guidelines of the amendment; a market maker is required to publish quotations for any listed security when it is responsible for more than 1 percent of the aggregate trading volume for that security. All superior prices that a market maker privately quotes through ECNs also have to be made public.

■ **ECN Amendment** – Under this, market makers and specialists are required to publicly display the price of any superior orders which are better than the quote placed by them, either by accounting for these orders in the public quote, or by making the private network publicly available by linking them to the major markets. ECNs are permitted to fulfil these obligations on behalf of market makers using its system by submitting its best bid/ask quotations to an SRO for inclusion into public quote displays.

Derivatives policy

In 1997, the SEC adopted market risk disclosure rules requiring reporting companies to disclose the policies used to account for derivatives and certain qualitative and quantitative information about market risk exposures. The SEC also amended the net capital rule to permit broker-dealers to employ theoretical option pricing models in determining net capital requirements for listed options and related positions.

Electronic document delivery policy

The SEC's 1996 release provided guidance on the use of electronic media by broker-dealers, transfer agents and investment advisers to fulfil their obligations to deliver certain information to customers but without sacrificing the investor protections provided by the federal securities laws. The SEC cautioned the regulated entities to take precautions to ensure the integrity, confidentiality and security of their clients' personal financial information, and to obtain client consent prior to delivering personal financial information electronically.

Automation Review Policy

In November 1989, the SEC issued its first Automation Review Policy (ARP), in which it stated that the SROs, on a voluntary basis, should establish comprehensive planning and assessment programs to determine systems capacity and vulnerability. In May 1991, the SEC issued its second Automation Review Policy.

In ARP II, the SEC set forth guidance concerning the nature of the independent reviews recommended in ARP I. The SROs were given guidelines for providing the SEC with information regarding automation developments or enhancements and system outages. These directions have ensured that currently all SROs have contingency and capacity plans, and have built in extra capacity for volatile trading days.

Just as with SROs, broker-dealers have also experienced operational problems caused by disasters and market volatility. The best example of this is that several broker-dealers' systems were disrupted following the explosions at the World Trade Center in September 2000. Online broker-dealers have also faced difficulties due to system outages and service failures and have also had difficulty in handling rapid increases in trading volumes. These system failures have the potential to disrupt the online operations of financial companies.

Electronic storage media The SEC amended its record retention rule to allow broker-dealers to use electronic storage media, such as CD-ROM and optical disk technology, to maintain their required records. This rule is not limited to electronic communications but includes all required records in whatever form they are originally produced. The amended rule does not specify the type of storage technology that may be used, but rather provides flexibility by setting out minimum standards that an electronic storage medium must satisfy to be considered an acceptable method of storage.

Retention of electronically generated communications The SEC provided guidance to broker-dealers about their obligations to retain email or internet communications. The broker-dealers may use the electronic medium for all sorts of communications to their customers as well as to the general public. But communications relating to the broker-dealers' business-related activity have to be compulsorily retained by broker-dealers.

Amendments to electronic communications

The SROs have adapted their rules and practices to deal with the use of electronic media, such as advertising on the internet and supervision of electronic communications by registered persons. In 1995, the SEC approved amendments to the NASD Rules of Fair Practice, broadening the definitions of "advertisements" and "sales literature" to specifically include electronic media and communications. Moreover, the Fair Practice Rules were amended to require supervisory approval of all advertising and sales literature prior to their use or filing with the NASD. SRO rules also require member firms to review all written communications such as correspondence, advertisements, sales literature and research reports with the public by registered representatives under their supervision.

Regulation NMS

In April 2005, the SEC adopted the new Regulation NMS (national market system). Regulation NMS has been designed to modernize the regulatory structure of the US equity markets and addresses four main topics:

1 **Order protection** (or prohibitions on "trade-through") – This requires trading centers to establish, maintain and enforce written policies and procedures designed to prevent the execution of trades at prices inferior to protected quotations displayed by other trading centers. To be protected, a quotation must be immediately and automatically accessible.

2 **Intermarket access rules** – This requires fair and non-discriminatory access to quotations, establishes a limit on access fees to harmonize the pric-

ing of quotations across different trading centers, and requires national securities exchanges and national securities associations to adopt, maintain and enforce rules that prohibit members from engaging in a pattern or practice of displaying quotations that lack or cross automated quotations.

3 **Sub-penny pricing rule** – This rule prohibits market participants from accepting, ranking or displaying orders, quotations or indications of interest in a pricing increment smaller than a penny, except for orders, quotations, or indications of interest that are priced at less than $1 per share.

4 **Market data rules** – These are amendments to the existing rules for promotion of a much wider and efficient distribution of market data.

The new Regulation NMS will facilitate the establishment of a national market system to link together the multiple individual markets that trade securities. By incorporating such technologies, the NMS is designed to achieve the objectives of efficient, competitive, fair and orderly markets that are in the public interest and protect investors. This new NMS is set to become effective from August 29, 2005.

The SEC actively monitors the state of technology in the markets and the effect of technological advances on both the industry as well as the SEC's regulatory program. The SEC has always tried to balance the need to develop more efficient methods of business practices while providing guidance to investors to efficiently use the technological developments in the system and also protecting investors from defrauds. Overall, recent technology advances have brought greater transparency, provided unprecedented opportunities for innovation and competition, facilitated tremendous increases in trading volume, and made possible the development of methods to reduce risk. At the same time, the rapid pace of technology driven changes to the markets have challenged and will continue to challenge the SEC to reevaluate and revise the manner in which it oversees the securities markets.

Regulation in Europe

The economic and political integration of the EU began with the signing of the Treaty of Rome in 1957. However, despite this Treaty, historically, securities regulation has been absent throughout the European markets, making the EU's efforts at regulation challenging to implement. The EU has been a union of sorts across the continent of various countries with different ideologies, weak internal regulatory bodies and, in some countries, even a culture of non-disclosure. This has made it even easier to manipulate the regulations.

The earlier Directives issued by the EU merely required Member States to meet common standards within their own borders. For example, the 1979 Admissions Directive required Member State legislation to establish baseline listing requirements for companies issuing securities, including requirements that the issuer has published financial statements for the preceding three years, the securities listed are freely negotiable, and the securities are sufficiently distributed to permit a market.

The Committee of European Securities Regulation (CESR) issued some Directives to unify the stock market across the various countries in the EU. A few significant Directives are discussed below:

■ **Information Directive** (1980) – This required that companies listed on any EU exchange file certain "listing particulars". These include the name of the person responsible for preparing the information required by the Directive and for auditing financial statements, the capitalization of the issuer, the issuer's business activities, the issuer's assets and liabilities, its financial position, profits and losses, the issuer's management and its prospects for the coming year.

- **Interim Reports Directive** (1982) – This required that all companies issuing stock publish biannual reports on activities, profits and losses.

- **Prospectus Directive** (1989) – This established requirements for what information companies must publish in a prospectus. The requirements include the terms of the offer, the nature of securities, withholding taxes, underwriting arrangements, transfer restrictions and pre-emptive rights, issuer's capitalization, issuer's business activities, issuer's material contracts, patents and licenses, legal proceedings, issuer's annual and interim financial statements, issuer's business trends and prospects of the current year.

- **The Mutual Funds Directive** (1985) – This set guidelines for supervision, structure, activities and disclosure requirements for mutual funds and also permitted marketing of mutual funds throughout the EU upon authorization by one Member State.

Initially, all these Directives were helpful in beginning to structure a more uniform system of regulation. However, the Directives did not facilitate or encourage cross-border transactions. Member States regulated the securities industry solely at the national level, requiring firms to adhere to the national standards existing in the Member State where the firms chose to conduct business. These arrangements left firms vulnerable to discriminatory regulations in foreign countries and subjected them to the high costs of obtaining authorization by several governments.

To alleviate these problems the CESR adopted the **Mutual Recognition Directive** in 1987, which represented a shift from commonality to reciprocity. This legislation applied to issuers of stock and mutual funds, and amended existing Directives. It required that where an issuer complied with the laws established by one Member State pursuant to an amended Directive that compliance would be sufficient to comply with the rules of other Member States. In other words, if an issuer's listing particulars were approved by a competent authority in one Member State, they must be recognized in other Member States without additional scrutiny.

Given the complexity and magnitude of the task, there are a number of national governments' regulatory authorities involved in the process. EU regulation has been slow but the CESR which was formed in 2001 has been instrumental in trying to unify the EU.

For unifying any cross-border market, the most important step is the unification of the banking system. The EU had a goal of implementing a common market by 1993. As the nations of Europe moved towards integrating their economies, the two models of financial regulation came into conflict. New EU laws needed either to choose between or somehow blend the two approaches.

The issue was settled by the 1989 **Second Banking Coordination Directive** and the 1993 **Investment Services Directive**. These granted European nations broad latitude in establishing their legal and regulatory framework for financial services. Financial firms were granted a "single passport" to operate throughout the EU, subject to the regulations of their home country. A bank domiciled in an EU country that permitted universal banking could conduct universal banking in another EU country that prohibited it. With France and Germany committed to universal banking, the single passport model effectively opened all Europe to universal banking. It also permitted Britain to maintain a separate regulatory framework for its non-bank securities firms.

The First Investment Services Directive (ISD)

Goals of establishing the ISD

The first ISD was adopted to foster the freedom of capital movement among EU members. The ISD protected the investors and facilitated the smooth functioning of capital markets by requiring mutual recognition of minimum standards for the activity of investment firms across Member States' borders, rather than by requiring strict harmonization of laws. It permits an investment firm to conduct business throughout the EU after obtaining authorization in just one Member State. The ISD enabled the extension of the notion of the "single market" in the financial services arena.

Another goal of the ISD was the prevention of protectionist regulatory discrimination against outsiders. Prior to implementation of the ISD, some Member States unfairly excluded foreign investment firms from competition.

The ISD also reduced the compliance costs for investment firms operating in the EU by requiring authorization only in one Member State. Prior to implementation of the ISD, investment firms were subject to the unnecessary financial burden imposed by having to seek approval in every Member State in which they wanted to conduct business.

The ISD is useful for anyone in the business of providing investment services. Such services include brokerage, dealing, market making, portfolio management, underwriting and distribution of securities, individual investment advice, and safekeeping and administration. The Directive's key provisions include Home State authorization, mutual recognition, prudential regulation, conduct-of-business rules and exchange membership for foreign investment firms.

Home State authorization is the process by which an investment firm obtains permission to provide services in the Member State in which it principally conducts business. It requires that the firm have a main office located in the Member State where it is seeking authorization and that the firm has sufficient initial capital.

Mutual recognition is the process by which firms receive permission to conduct business in Member States other than the ones that have granted them authorization.

The prudential rules established by the ISD prescribed specific safeguards that firms must have in place in order to ensure full compliance with the regulations. These included sound administrative and accounting procedures, controls and safeguards over electronic data processing, adequate internal control mechanisms, segregation of accounts, records of all transactions and procedures to minimize the risk of conflicts of interest. Firms also must obtain information from clients about their financial positions and investment experiences and objectives, avoid conflicts of interest and comply with all regulatory requirements.

Finally, the ISD required that Member States allow investment firms to become members of their stock exchanges and also provide more transparency in stock trading.

Shortcomings in the Implementation of ISD

Upon adoption, the ISD was hailed as the cornerstone of EU securities regulation and was said to complete "the final piece of framework" legislation needed for the creation of a single market in the financial services industry. However, the ISD was unable to complete the EU securities regulation due to various shortfalls in the system.

The first problem was slow implementation. Even at the end of 1998, not even half the total number of Member States had adopted the ISD norms. The second problem was that regulatory discrimination was not eradicated completely even where Member States complied with the ISD. Some Member States had implemented special rules to grant certain concessions to their local exchanges. This led to discrimination. Another short-coming was that the ISD set up the framework to allow investment firms to conduct business not in all Member States, but only in those Member States in which they have established branch offices.

The framework of EU securities regulation faced additional challenges such as the emergence of alternative trading systems, the uncertainty of redress for individual investors, the lack of uniform taxation and a large disparity in pricing. Each of these issues presented an obstacle to the creation of a fully integrated capital market.

We can sum up the failure of the ISD by quoting what Roberta Karmel, professor of international business law at Brooklyn Law School has to say: "transferring oversight of the self-regulatory process to fifteen different national securities regulators will not result in a pan-European securities market but will compound the problems of a fragmented system for the trading and regulation of securities."

Investment Services Directive 2

Inadequacies in the ISD 1 were identified quite quickly and revision of it began as early as the mid-1990s. The broad discretionary scope for the national interpretation of individual provisions and the problems with the application of national law to conduct business rules emerged as stumbling blocks to capital market integration and thus to cross-border securities trading. Moreover, the trading environment itself had changed and consequently the demands of regulation also would change. The alternative trading mechanisms had also gained acceptance and were operating quite efficiently alongside the registered stock exchanges. The stock exchanges themselves had altered the trading systems and rules to beat the competition from the ATSs.

The market structure had also shifted and most member exchanges of the EU were strongly focusing on the issue of whether the concentration of orders in a central marketplace was preferred over the more open ATSs. However, France was pushing for the "concentration rule", whereby the EU Member States could issue regulations specifying that orders by retail investors for securities listed on the domestic stock market could only be traded on the exchange. This also had opposition from exchanges, especially the LSE, which had developed a competitive system for cross-border trading.

The ISD 2 was formally adopted in April 2004 and is to be implemented by April 2006. The aim of the new ISD 2 regulation is to achieve a Directive that better protects investors and integrity, while promoting efficient and integrated markets. It contains stronger rules regarding the operation of investment firms (for example, conflicts of interest) and their relationships with clients (for example, best execution). For regulated markets, the new regulation provides for more harmonized rules relating to organizational requirements, the operators of the market, and admission of instruments to trading and transparency.

The ISD 2 also contains elaborate provisions on supervisory authorities, in particular concerning the designation in each Member State of a competent authority and its powers and resources. The ISD 2 contains transparency requirements for regulated markets and investment firms, the latter including ATSs (or multilateral trading facilities – MTFs) and broker-dealers.

For regulated markets, a comprehensive transparency regime will apply. As for pre-trade information, regulated markets will have to make public part of their order book if they are order-driven, while quote-driven markets' traders will have to publish some of their bid and ask quotes. With regard to post-trade transparency, regulated markets will have to publish prices, volumes and times of all equity trades. Only large block trades will be exempted from this rule. Even if the trades are executed on the ATSs or MTFs, they will be subject to the same transparency rules as when executed on the stock exchange trading system.

Commodity derivatives have been included on the list of financial instruments, bringing EU commodities markets and market participants within the scope of the ISD for the first time. The restriction of scope in the case of derivatives to instruments with cash settlement (that is, cash payment of the difference instead of physical delivery) has been retained.

The introduction of a definition of professional clients in contrast to private clients, in conjunction with the amendments to the rules of conduct, constitutes one of the major amendments of ISD 2. It formally categorizes clients for the first time, on the basis of institutional criteria (credit institution, pension funds and the like), or in the case of corporate investors, on the basis of threshold values. Categorization as a professional client entails a lower level of investor protection and hence the possibility for investment firms to conduct business with these customers under reduced information and advisory obligations.

The EU Commission has acknowledged the presence of internalization of order execution and accepted the fact that transparency rules cannot be applied to internalized trades. It therefore proposes two requirements for broker-traders internalizing orders:

- **Client Limit Order Display Rule** – This will require investment firms to publish those limit orders (instructions to trade at best price, but not worse than specified limit) that they are unwilling or unable to execute themselves immediately. Such unexecuted limit orders are interesting from a price point of view and the rule's aim is to ensure that the information reaches the market. However, it allows a number of exceptions. If clients request orders not to be disclosed, investment firms will not be obliged to publish. Also, the rule does allow exceptions for large transactions.

- **Quote Disclosure Rule** – Under this, investment firms that run a trading book are required to publish the terms (bid and ask quotes) at which they are ready to trade typical retail transactions in liquid equities. By limiting the rule to retail trades and liquid equities, the EU Commission has tried to ensure that the rule will not impede larger transactions.

Loose ends

ISD 2 aims to promote capital market integration in the EU so that it meets the requirements of the evolving market – a well-proportioned, regulated capital market enjoying the confidence of investors and issuers. However, it does contain regulations that clearly run counter to the creation of a single and competitive financial market in the EU. The extensive initiatives to develop alternative trading systems that have sprung up in recent years are testament to strong innovative strengths and readiness. But they also point up inefficiencies in existing systems that need to be remedied and show that investors have needs which are not satisfied by traditional trading systems. As of now the ATSs have a very limited market penetration. The proposed transparency regulations would seriously hamper – if not entirely frustrate – market participants' attempts to provide investors with more economical and varied services. The ATSs or ECNs are cheaper alternatives to trading on the more time-consuming as well as more expensive traditional exchange trading systems. Imposing regulations on the ATSs will make trading on these systems expensive.

The aim should be to guarantee customers free choice of execution. Theoretically, it is possible to vet providers at any time, although we must not forget that operators are already regulated, either as banks or investment firms. To improve the competitiveness of the European capital market, scope should be created for innovation and customer focus. Both issuers and investors should be allowed to benefit from the advantages of a single integrated European market with a single currency (euro) for operating throughout the EU.

Despite the significant improvements in ISD 2, some more loose ends need to be tied up by the Commission. ISD 2 does not go far enough to introduce measures designed to reduce the high cost of cross-border clearing and settlement.

There are also a few gaps in ISD 2. However, just as regulations in the USA have evolved, so will the EU regulatory body evolve with developments in the market. Gradually, all the gaps will be filled. But to reach that stage all Member States will have to conform to the regulations set up by the EU.

The Future of the Pan-European Capital Market

Although it is difficult to visualize the integration of over 40 national exchanges and as many local regulators in the EU, it is not such a knotty scenario. Currently though it appears difficult mainly because the responsibilities are different and, in some cases, enforcement is weak.

Adopting a uniform accounting system

Clearly, the adoption of International Accounting Standards will improve the functioning of the securities markets only when they are enforced. Currently, not many companies look at the pan-European market as a unified market for raising capital due to a number of regulatory barriers. However, the EU Commission is in the process of developing important legislative measures to ease cross-border IPOs. These proposals include EU Directives on a single public offering prospectus, the prudent supervision of financial conglomerates and insider trading and market manipulation.

Integrating clearing and settlement systems

Integrating the clearing and settlement systems is also an important function for integrating the capital markets. The fragmentation of clearing and settlement systems leads to excessive cross-border trading costs and is consequently a major impediment to market consolidation. In this direction, some horizontal integration among the clearing agencies has been highlighted in the previous chapter.

Enforcing publication of uniform financial statements

The EU stock exchanges should enforce the issue of a standard financial statement by all companies listed on themselves. This will lead to a clearer understanding of each other's market region and consequently increase cross-border trades. This in turn will force integration among the clearing and settlement agencies, leading to the creation of a pan-European exchange.

We can conclude with what Dr. Patrick Dixon wrote in *The Times* (19 October 1998): "National stock exchanges cannot possibly survive. The London Stock Market will disappear altogether, as will every other national exchange in Europe to create a pan-European Exchange."

The Shape of Things to Come

Technology has eased cross-border trading and it is technically possible for an Australian investor to trade via the internet on the European or American exchanges. However, although physical distances have eroded due to the advances in technology, regulations make it difficult to trade cross-border as efficiently.

The different regulatory authorities across various countries are striving hard to develop and integrate the regulations across national stock exchanges. But the road ahead for a unified regulatory system is strewn with problems. Currently, the regulatory authorities are attempting to clear these problems and integrate the regulations so that the hypothetical Australian investor can trade anywhere in the world from his/her home.

Once European stock exchanges integrate trading, clearing and settlement and also have one regulatory body governing them, the next natural forward integration will be integrating with the American and Asian stock exchanges. This process may be smoother and much faster. Already a few European and American exchanges on their own have trading links and technological hubs with a few prominent stock exchanges in the Asia-Pacific region.

Along with the regulatory framework, the banking sector also has to be integrated, because payments will also have to made for closing a transaction and currencies differ from country to country. The European region has succeeded in integrating the currency with the introduction of the euro.

However, it will not be feasible to develop one currency for the whole world. The next best alternative will be to develop a well-integrated global banking sector. This in turn will require a well-developed banking regulatory framework. Of course a well-developed banking sector is also needed for the development of efficient clearing and settlement systems and helps in setting up STP of clearing and settlement. Generally, only a handful of well-developed national stock exchanges have STP of trading.

If the banking sector is well regulated, then currency conversion can be done with minimal effort and instantly. And then our hypothetical Australian investor can trade anywhere in the world and clear his/her transaction and pay/receive his/her dues through his/her local banker in Australian dollars. But the local banker will settle the transaction with its foreign counterpart in the local currency of the trading exchange or trading system.

CASE STUDIES

Euronext N.V.

Euronext N.V. is the first genuinely cross-border exchange organization in Europe. It provides services for regulated stock and derivatives markets in Belgium, France, the Netherlands and Portugal as well as the UK (derivatives only). It is Europe's leading stock exchange based on trading volumes on the central order book.

A consolidation of five exchanges

Euronext was formed on September 22, 2000, when the Amsterdam, Brussels and Paris exchanges merged to form Euronext N.V., a holding company incorporated under Dutch law. In January 2002, Euronext acquired LIFFE – the London International Financial Futures and Options Exchange. Subsequently, in February 2002, Bolsa de Valores de Lisboa e Porto (BVLP), the Portuguese stock exchange, joined Euronext.

For regulatory reasons, notably regarding the admission of securities to listing and tender offers, as well as to respect each member market's domestic environment, the five market operators – now wholly owned subsidiaries of Euronext N.V. – continue to exist separately. With the exception of LIFFE, which retains its name, the other exchanges have been renamed as Euronext Amsterdam N.V., Euronext Brussels S.A./N.V., Euronext Lisbon S.A. and Euronext Paris S.A. Euronext is more than a market or a group of cash and derivatives markets. It is a company whose subsidiaries organize, operate and provide access to market issuers, intermediaries and investors across borders, integrating trading and clearing operations for derivatives and cash products on regulated as well as non-regulated markets.

A single well-integrated trading platform

Euronext is integrating its markets across Europe to provide users with a single market that is very broad, highly liquid and extremely cost-effective. In 2004, it completed the integration of its five subsidiaries and migrated its markets to harmonized IT platforms for cash trading (NSC), derivatives (LIFFE CONNECT) and clearing. Euronext's development and integration model generates synergies by incorporating the individual strengths and assets of each local market, proving that the most successful way to merge European exchanges is to apply global vision at a local level.

Diversified revenue base

Euronext has diversified sources of revenues, which protect it against fluctuations in the financial markets. Developments such as the acquisition of LIFFE (the London-based derivatives market) in 2002 and the merger of Euronext's subsidiary Clearnet with the London Clearing House in 2003 have made the Group's derivatives markets and European clearing activities more efficient, providing benefits for the entire European financial community.

Evolution of the Exchange

A exchange formed by mergers ...

Euronext was founded on September 22, 2000 through the merger of the Amsterdam exchange (AEX), the Brussels exchange (BXS) and the Paris Bourse SBF, now known as Euronext Amsterdam, Euronext Brussels and Euronext Paris respectively.

In December 2001, Euronext reached an agreement on a full merger with the Portuguese exchange BVLP, which led to the creation of Euronext Lisbon in January 2002.

Euronext acquired LIFFE (London International Financial Futures and Options Exchange) following an agreed offer initiated in October 2001. LIFFE retains its original name, and consequently Euronext.liffe has become a part of the Euronext group.

The exchange made its IPO on July 5, 2001. Its shares were priced at €24, valuing the company at €2.8bn.

Since its inception on September 22, 2000, Euronext has been moving towards operational integration by stages. Euronext Amsterdam, Euronext Brussels and Euronext Paris have been linked to a single cash trading platform (NSC) for cash products since October 29, 2001, while Euronext Lisbon was linked in November 2003. By November 2004, all five subsidiaries had a single integrated derivatives trading platform, LIFFE Connect.

... and acquisitions

In 2003, Euronext bought the London Clearing House and merged it with Clearnet to form LCH.Clearnet. Euronext has a 41.5 percent stake of the equity and a 24.9 percent stake in the voting rights in LCH.Clearnet. LCH.Clearnet is Europe's leading provider of clearing and CCP services. Since November 2003, all cash and derivatives transactions on the Euronext are cleared through LCH.Clearnet.

Trades executed on Euronext's markets are settled through Euroclear, which provides settlements for both cash as well as derivatives products.

Part owner of a well-developed clearing system – ATOS-Euronext

Euronext's trading and clearing systems are developed and marketed by ATOS-Euronext, a 50:50 joint venture between Euronext and Atos Origin, a Euronext Paris listed company that is also Europe's leading information technology provider. ATOS-Euronext provides technological solutions for cash settlement, exchange trading, retail banking, clearing houses, e-commerce, insurance and electronic payment and has clients all over the world. By working with ATOS-Euronext, Euronext has access to a large international pool of technological skills and resources at a competitive price while retaining a higher degree of control than can be obtained through contracting work out.

Major stakeholder of GL Trade – leading provider of electronic front to back office tracking solutions

Euronext is a major shareholder of GL Trade, the world's leading provider of electronic front to back office tracking solutions, with over 3500 clients spread across 105 markets and 23 offices in five continents. This strategic investment has put Euronext in a position to benefit from the complementary business built up by a worldwide provider of front to back office e-trading solutions, at a time when deregulation makes room for alternative trading platforms and related components.

Majority holder of Powernext – regulated power exchange

In July 2001, Powernext, France's only regulated power exchange, was formed jointly by BNP-Paribas, ELIA (Belgium transmission system operator), EDF, Electrabel, RTE (French transmission system operator), Société Générale and TotalFinaElf under the leadership of Euronext. Euronext is the majority shareholder with a 34 percent equity stake. Powernext has become a leading benchmark for energy prices.

Powernext SA is a multilateral trading facility in charge of managing an optional and anonymous organized exchange offering:

■ Day-ahead contracts for the management of volume risk

■ Medium-term contracts for the management of price risk.

Euronext – An Open Architecture

Euronext is not only a merged entity, it is also an open venture. It is open to new mergers, alliances and other joint ventures with other exchanges and market operators. Since it was founded five years ago, Euronext has been committed to promoting the integration and consolidation of Europe's capital markets and increasing the efficiency of cross-border trading. It has developed a business structure based on an open architecture that supports the integration of various markets on the same technological platform. By transferring its settlement activities, Euronext has championed open back office architecture and supported the development of independent clearing and settlement organizations that can be used by any exchange.

Technological Integration – Basis for Cross-border Reorganization

Euronext uses technology as the basis for its growth and cross-border business strategy. The ambitious project of integrating cash and derivatives trading on a single trading system across the different countries is itself an achievement. Today, Euronext's markets are supported by two common platforms – one for cash trading (NSC) and another for derivatives trading (LIFFE CONNECT), which interface with LCH.Clearnet's clearing systems. Euronext minimized the disruption that the migrations could create for users by working in close consultation with IT specialists (AtosEuronext and Euronext.liffe Market Solutions) and customers at every stage of the process. Euronext now gives customers access to a wider market and a larger range of trading products at lower costs. By harmonizing its systems, Euronext has been able to reduce the number of systems it has to maintain. This has simplified the rollout of new releases and consequently increased operational efficiency, while reducing its expenses on this count.

Euronext – A Consolidated Exchange

The consolidation of Euronext's cash and derivatives markets on an integrated trading platform has created a more efficient and liquid market, lowered costs and simplified trading. It has enhanced the visibility of listed companies. The integrated system also led to a reduction in average trading fees which in turn has triggered a lowering of fees on the other European exchanges.

Cross-border Integration – Promotes Cooperation

Euronext is a fully integrated, international organization of multinational teams. Its business activities are organized into three cross-border, product-based strategic business units (SBUs). The three SBUs are:

- Cash and listing
- Derivatives
- Information services.

Each of the SBUs is highly cohesive, operates under a single chain of command and has the responsibility for the activities and staff at all Euronext's marketplaces, irrespective of the location of the offices. Each SBU focuses on providing core customer services and achieving the Group's business objective of improved financial performance.

The SBUs are responsible for cost control and are structured in a way that maximizes the quality of customer service, marketing campaigns and the Group's investment policy. The structure is designed to boost team spirit among staff and create an international, service-focused culture that respects the diversity of Euronext's local marketplaces. The SBUs have been able to efficiently handle the complexity of the cultural and legal environment in which the Group operates.

The SBUs are assisted by cross-border Group support departments – Finance, Human Resources, Legal, Regulation, Compliance and European Affairs, Corporate Information Systems, Business Strategy and other support departments. These Group support departments coordinate matters and ensure coherence and consistency throughout the organization.

Harmonized Regulatory Framework

While Euronext integrated the trading platforms, it also introduced a harmonized rule book across all its markets. The harmonized rule book has reduced the compliance burden on users and thereby reduced costs. Euronext has harmonized its rules and procedures by a process of increasingly close cooperation between the regulators of each of the financial markets in each of the EU member states where it operates – the AFM (Autoriteint Financiele Markten, the Netherlands), the AMF (Autorité des Marchés Financiers, France), the CBFA (Commission Bancaire, Financiere et des Assurances/Commissie voor het Bank, Financie en Assurantiewezen, Belgium), the CMVM (Comissao do Mercado de Valores Mobiliiarios, Portugal) and the FSA (Financial Services Authority, UK). The first three regulators adopted a common approach and drew up a memorandum of understanding (MoU) in March 2001 regarding the coordinated regulation and supervision of Euronext and the regulated markets it operates. In March 2002, the MoU was extended to include the CMVM. It was followed by a second MoU between Euronext's regulators and the FSA for the derivatives markets.

Market Expansion

Euronext follows an open structure and pursues a policy of obtaining recognition on major non-European markets too. To expand its international base, the exchange has obtained no-action letters from the US regulatory bodies to permit US investors to trade on the derivatives exchange, Euronext.liffe, and trade options and futures contracts on Euronext Paris.

Euronext also follows a policy of cross-membership and cross-access agreements with other exchanges that enables its members to trade securities listed on other markets and vice versa. The exchange has agreements with the Swiss exchange, the Luxembourg exchange, OMX and the Warsaw exchange.

- **Swiss Exchange:** Five Swiss members have become active on the Paris securities markets since a cross-membership and cross-trading agreement was signed with the predecessor Euronext Paris in March 1999.

- **Bourse de Luxembourg:** A cross-membership and cross-trading agreement giving the Bourse de Luxembourg's members access to Euronext's markets in Amsterdam, Brussels and Paris was signed in November 2000. Euronext Lisbon is now party to the agreement.

- **OMX:** In November 2000, Euronext signed a cross-membership and cross-access agreement with the Helsinki exchange which has subsequently merged with OM exchanges to form OMX. While OMX members can trade on all Euronext cash products, OMX also establishes an access point at Euronext, offering access for Euronext members to the Finnish stock market.

- **Warsaw Stock Exchange:** A cross-membership and cross-trading agreement was signed in February 2002 with Euronext Amsterdam, Euronext Brussels and Euronext Paris. The agreement, which now includes Euronext Lisbon, has been finalized and reciprocal technical access is now being implemented for members.

Integrated and open, Euronext's model is primarily designed to be efficient. The model has generated major cost savings for Euronext, bringing down its fixed cost base. This has resulted in lowering the fees for both cash and derivatives trading, further reinforcing Euronext's competitive position.

Competition in the derivatives sector in 2004 targeted US markets. Eurex US was launched in February 2004, offering US dollar denominated derivatives and equity index products. Euronext.liffe entered the US market one month later with the launch of three-month eurodollar futures and option contracts. Since the cost of trading on the Euronext was much lower than that offered by the US exchanges, the major US exchanges – CME and CBOT – had to reduce their pricing structure to match Euronext's trading price.

Euronext.liffe Acquires Cscreen

In April 2005, Euronext.liffe acquired CScreen Ltd., the provider of CScreen, a leading pre-trade price discovery platform for wholesale equity derivatives, from Cinnober Financial Technology AB.

This acquisition will enable Euronext.liffe to offer its customers STP facilities for the first time, from pre-trade price discovery to post-trade booking and administration. This acquisition will automate the existing manual processes inherent in over-the-counter transactions, giving customers a flexible, secure, simple and significantly cheaper way of conducting their wholesale derivatives business.

Alternext – A Market for Small and Mid-cap Companies

Euronext began a separate market for small and mid-cap companies from May 2005 called Alternext. Alternext is an innovative market solution for medium-sized companies seeking to finance growth and gain access to capital markets. It is an exchange-regulated market that offers simplified access to financial markets and streamlined listing requirements from small and medium-sized companies from every sector of the economy, while ensuring compliance with the rules on investor disclosure and control of financial information.

Small and medium-sized companies play a vital role in the European economy, but only a small percentage of them are publicly traded. As the Eurozone's leading exchange, Euronext is reiterating its commitment to help these companies grow at a time when EU regulations are imposing tougher requirements on registered markets.

Listing and trading on the Alternext is much simpler. Companies wanting to list on the Alternext can make an IPO of just €2.5m or the company can also make a private placement of €5m with five or more qualified investors within the two years preceding the listing application.

Disclosure norms have also been tailored to suit the structure of small and medium-sized companies. The companies listed on Alternext have to make periodic disclosures like annual and half-yearly accounts and report other price-sensitive information to ensure that the investors are well protected.

A new category of market participant, the listing sponsor, has been created for the Alternext market. These Euronext recognized and approved intermediaries, whose presence is mandatory, will provide applicants with specialist expertise for a period of two years. The listing sponsor has two roles to play:

■ Advise the applicant to prepare for an Alternext listing

■ Support and guide the issuer throughout its life as a listed company, ensuring that the company complies with disclosure requirements.

Alternext offers two complementary and transparent trading procedures to enhance liquidity in stocks with a smaller free float. The trading day is organized around a market-making session followed by an end-of-day auction. The presence of market makers (although optional) enhances the liquidity via continuous display of bid-ask spreads for minimum quantities; it also facilitates block trades and increases the number of investors specialized in mid-caps. Investors can choose how their order is to be executed and the spreads and prices are displayed in order to ensure transparency in the market.

Alternext is beneficial for all. Issuers have easy access to capital markets, investors have new investment opportunities, issuing companies have the opportunity to increase visibility and build long-term relationships with sponsors, brokers and bankers. Finally, the venture capitalists also have a natural exit route for their holdings.

Proposes to Acquire LSE

In December 2004 Euronext announced that it was considering making a cash offer for the LSE. Since then there have been a series of meetings between the two exchanges regarding the key aspects of a combined venture. Euronext submitted a filing to the Office of Fair Trading in January 2005. So far nothing concrete has emerged. Earlier Deutsche Börse had also made a preconditional unsolicited cash offer for the LSE, which was rejected by the LSE.

If the deal goes through, the LSE, like the LIFFE, will have a separate, independent board with an independent chairman. The LSE would continue to be a recognized investment exchange (RIE) regulated solely by the FSA, and Euronext will provide a solid long-term commitment that the LSE will remain a UK RIE. Euronext has significant work experience working with multiple regulators and, specifically through the acquisition of LIFFE, has a proven track record in the UK.

Euronext will continue to offer transparent and efficient trading with open post-trade architecture. The combined group will adopt a unitary single tier board structure consistent with accepted UK practice and the highest international corporate governance standards, including the Combined Code. Euronext would seek a dual primary listing for its shares in London and Paris.

As per Euronext's projection, the combination of the LSE with Euronext will provide immediate benefits to the users of the LSE in the following manner:

- 10 percent overall reduction in current tariffs for UK cash trading on the central order book, with a commitment to continued reductions

- 10 percent reduction in information services fees for customers subscribing to a combined data package.

The combination of Euronext and the LSE will represent a major consolidation for the European markets and create a platform for the leading global exchange of the future. If it goes through, the pace of consolidation between other European exchanges will hasten and we will witness a truly global consolidation process.

OMX AB

OMX is the best example of how the futuristic stock exchanges will be. It has many firsts to its credit. It operates a fully integrated cash and derivatives market in the Nordic and Baltic region. The exchange is the epitome of a smooth cross-border trading platform. The OMX Exchange division comprises the integrated Nordic/Baltic marketplace that offers customers access to approximately 80 percent of the Nordic and Baltic securities markets. The division includes the exchanges in Copenhagen, Stockholm, Helsinki, Tallinn, Riga, Vilnius (Lithuania) (all exchanges owned by OMX) as well as the stock exchanges in Oslo and Iceland. It operates the common trading platform SAXESS across these exchanges. It provides customer benefits, such as harmonized Nordic and Baltic trading rules as well as one access point to the eight different markets. As at the end of May 2005, the OMX Exchange has 677 companies listed on it and 144 trading members.

OMX is a relatively new exchange – it only began its operations in September 2003 – but it was born from established parent exchanges. OMX was created by the merger of the HEX and OM. This merger created a new company with a clear vision of an integrated securities market in Northern Europe and a stronger position as a global technology provider.

OMX has two main divisions – OMX Technology and OMX Exchange. The OMX Exchange operates Northern Europe's largest securities market. OMX Technology is the world's leading provider of transaction technology, processing and outsourcing solutions to global financial markets.

Evolution of the Exchange

Although OMX has only been in existence since September 2003, with the merger of HEX and OM, these two exchanges have been in existence for a long time.

The evolution of the Helsinki Exchange

The Helsinki Stock Exchange (HEX) began operating in 1912 as an informal association catering to business needs of broker-traders. In 1984 it became a cooperative society. The Co-operative Helsinki Stock Exchange was a non-profit organization, promoting its members' business by maintaining an unbiased marketplace for securities trading with ancillary services. The HEX was a progressive exchange, adapting to the various changes in technological development. In April 1990, the exchange replaced the open outcry trading system with the Helsinki Stock Exchange Automated Trading and Information System.

In 1995, the Co-operative Helsinki Stock Exchange became a joint stock company. In 1997, the Central Share Register of Finland, the Helsinki Stock Exchange Settlement Operations, the Helsinki Money Market Center and the Association of Book-entry Securities were merged to form the Finnish Central Securities Depository.

In 1997, the cash and derivatives marketplaces, the Helsinki Stock Exchange Ltd and SOM Ltd merged to become HEX Ltd, the Helsinki Stock and Derivatives Exchange Settlement Company, that is, the Helsinki Exchanges.

In November 1998, the Helsinki Exchanges announced a strategic plan for establishing a globally competitive marketplace, based on an independent national marketplace and international cooperation. As a part of this strategy, the Helsinki Exchanges and the CSD merged into the new HEX Group (Helsinki Exchanges Group plc). In 2001, the name of the exchange was changed to HEX plc.

The evolution of the OM exchange

OM was launched in 1985 and developed Northern Europe's first derivatives exchange. OM developed derivatives trading on Swedish equity options. In 1986, the OM index was introduced and OM developed clearing operations, taking on counterparty risk, a service to which it owes much of its success. OM was the first exchange to be demutualized and enlist on the stock exchange in 1987.

The exchange's order-based electronic trading system, Stockholm Automated Exchange (SAX), was launched in 1989. SAX automatically executes buy and sell orders and enables members to be connected from anywhere in the world. In 1990, OM developed and sold the world's first electronic exchange system for derivatives trading. In 1991, the Stockholm Bond Exchange was launched.

In 1997, the NOREX Alliance was formed between the Copenhagen and Stockholm exchanges (later joined by Iceland and Norway). In 1998, OM acquired the Stockholm Stock Exchange and merged it with itself. In 2000, OM launched UK Power Exchange (UKPX) – the UK's first electricity exchange.

In 2002, OM and the LSE formed EDX London, a trading and clearing equity derivatives exchange that commenced trading in 2003.

The merger

OM was the largest stockholder of HEX with a 15.6 percent stake. In May 2003, the boards of both exchanges decided to merge. The merger was effected through an offer by OM to issue 2.5 new shares of OM as against each share held by the stockholders of HEX. In addition, OM offered HEX warrant holders a cash consideration of €5.90. The offer was fully subscribed and OM acquired all the shares of HEX.

OMHEX formed in 2003 ...

In September 2003, OM and HEX merged to form OMHEX, the largest securities market in Northern Europe and a leading provider of marketplace solutions for the financial and energy markets. The post-merger entity had 490 listed companies, of which 297 were from OM.

Since the merger, OMHEX has emerged as the largest securities market in Northern Europe. It has integrated the Nordic and Baltic marketplace for securities and derivatives, giving customers access to 80 percent of the Nordic securities market. OMHEX is a fully automatic and integrated exchange, offering its customers the entire gamut of trading, clearing and settlement and depository functions. Having being in the business of providing trading system solutions to exchanges all over the world, the trading system of OMHEX is very efficient.

... and renamed OMX in 2004

In August 2004, the exchange renamed itself OMX. The company's new brand strategy is a simplified brand structure, with all operations affiliated to one master brand, OMX. The two divisions of OMX AB were renamed OMX Technology and OMX Exchanges from OM Technology and HEX Integrated Markets respectively.

Business Divisions

OMX has two main divisions – OMX Technology and OMX Exchange. Through OMX Exchange, OMX operates the securities market in Northern Europe. OMX Technology is the world's leading provider of transaction technology, processing and outsourcing solutions to global financial markets.

OMX Technology Division

This division includes OM's former technology operations as well as HEX's previous IT-related operations, and offers its clients three tiers of service:

1   It may solely develop and provide systems solutions. In this case, the licence fee that OMX Technology receives is mostly fixed but it can also be volume-based. The division is also likely to receive continuing support revenue.

2   It may take on responsibility for the operation of the systems solutions provided to the client – here it will generate recurring revenue.

3   It may take an equity stake in a business such as an exchange, and in doing so take on part of the business operations as a partner or owner. In this case, the division directly participates in trading revenues, largely dependent on volumes.

The OMX Technology division has three main business areas:

Banks and brokers: Provides business solutions and operational services for banks and brokerage firms.

Financial markets: Provides systems solutions for exchanges, clearing organizations and CSDs.

Global services: Provides systems operational services primarily for exchanges, clearing organizations and CSDs.

OMX technology has been a technical pioneer in many market sectors and has distinct advantages over its competitors. It provides a broad range of products and services that deliver integrated and complete solutions. The systems solutions have open architecture systems and facilitate integration between different types of systems and markets.

Product Development

The technology division creates value for its customers. It is at the forefront of technological development in its field. The exchange's technology division invests extensively in research and development to develop core competence within the company, while securing its position as market leader. Development is as much about creating new products as it is about adding new functionality to existing platforms and products.

Financial Market Solutions

The exchange has established a position as a market leader in providing systems solutions for exchanges, clearing houses and CSDs.

OMX Technology's two trading solutions – CLICK and SAXESS – operate in 27 global exchanges. Major CLICK customers include the American Stock Exchange, the Australian Stock Exchange, Korea

Futures and Borsa Italiana. SAXESS is used by all member exchanges of the Nordic exchange alliance NOREX.

In 2002, OM launched TYZER – an exchange system for smaller exchanges – and TSP – an outsourcing solution aimed at the same customer category.

SECUR – its clearing solution for clearing derivatives – is used by over 10 exchanges and clearing houses worldwide, including the Hong Kong and Stockholm Exchanges.

OMX Technology has also developed EXIGO CSD, an automated CSD system, and CLICK XT, a new integrated trading platform for equities and derivatives trading. Many exchanges are using these automated systems.

Bank and Broker Services

OMX Technology's bank and broker services provide largely automated integrated solutions within international trading, customer trading and internet trading for retail clients, regardless of currency or security type.

Global Services

Its global services offer a variety of operational services targeted at companies operating on the financial and energy markets that need mission-critical systems solutions, such as exchanges and clearing houses.

OMX Exchange Division

The OMX Exchange division was created through the merger of OM and HEX. The division includes the equity and derivatives exchanges in Stockholm, Helsinki, Tallinn, Riga, Vilnius (Lithuania) as well as the CSDs in Finland, Estonia and Latvia. This division has four business areas.

Cash Markets

Cash markets comprise equity trading including information sales and listing operations at the Stockholm and Helsinki Exchanges.

Derivatives Markets

The derivatives markets comprise derivatives trading and clearing operations at the Stockholm and Helsinki Exchanges, as well as cooperations mainly with Eurex and EDX London.

Settlement and Depository

Settlement and depository include the Finnish CSD, which provides clearing, settlement and depository services for equities and fixed income products.

Baltic Operations

Baltic operations include the stock exchanges, CSDs and the operation of the national funded pension account registers in Estonia and Latvia.

Consolidation and Integration of the OMX

The exchanges in OMX's home markets in the Nordic/ Baltic region are one of OMX's most important assets and the cornerstone of its business model. By operating and integrating these exchanges efficiently, OMX gains the necessary size, knowledge base and reference markets it needs to develop systems.

Uniform trading platform for all eight exchanges

The exchange has implemented a uniform trading platform SAXESS in all eight exchanges that it operates. This has created a well-integrated marketplace in the Nordic/Baltic region. The exchange is integrated both horizontally as well as vertically. The objective of an integrated market is to strengthen the region's competitive edge – and thereby the competitive edge of OMX Exchange's customers – by offering listing, trading, clearing and settlement based on common infrastructure, information dissemination and harmonized rules. This will help investors increasingly to regard the Nordic/Baltic region as a single market.

Integrated derivatives exchange

OMX successfully integrated the Finnish and Swedish derivatives markets, through the launch of the common derivatives trading platform CLICK XT for the Finnish market through one access point, to trade Finnish and Swedish derivatives products on the same platform and benefit from one rule book and a single membership.

Horizontally, integration is in the form of a common technical platform for the different local exchanges and their rule books as well as the development of a common platform for the Nordic and Baltic CSDs. Since the merger with the Copenhagen Stock Exchange, OMX offers access to approximately 80 percent of the Nordic/Baltic stock market. All the Nordic exchanges now have common membership requirements and trading rules for their exchange members.

With regard to trading, the exchanges within OMX Exchanges constitute the seventh largest stock exchange and the third largest derivatives exchange in Europe.

Owns a CSD	OMX-owned Finnish Central Securities Depository and VPC, the Swedish equivalent, merged in November 2004 to form the Nordic Central Securities Depository. This has created a strong joint CSD group within the Nordic region. This has led to strong vertical integration for the exchange.
Plans to start CCP	OMX is striving to create the prerequisites for the introduction of a pan-Nordic organization for CCP clearing for equity trading. Nordic CCP clearing will make securities administration more secure and efficient. It will also secure Nordic competitiveness, since CCP clearing is a natural component at bigger stock exchanges and of great interest to international members.
	A step towards market harmonization was taken when the exchanges in Stockholm, Helsinki, Tallinn and Riga implemented the information distribution system TARGIN.
Trading cooperations	The Linked Exchanges and Clearing (LEC) was set up in cooperation with the OMX Exchange, London, Oslo and Copenhagen for the trading and clearing of derivatives. The OMX Exchange also has a cooperation agreement with the German derivatives exchange Eurex. The volume of the Finnish derivatives contracts traded on the Eurex is very high. Further, OMX is also a part-owner of the EDX London derivatives exchange, which through LEC offers market participants trading in Nordic equity derivatives and local clearing.
Uniform industry classification standards followed on all exchanges on the Nordic/Baltic securities	As part of the integration of the Nordic and Baltic securities markets, all exchanges under OMX have begun using the same Global Industry Classification Standard for classifying listed securities since July, 2005. A common Nordic/Baltic industry classification improves the international comparability of the listed

companies and provides companies with a clearly defined and larger peer group.

An alternative market for smaller companies to be set up

The exchange is to set up an alternative marketplace for smaller companies by the end of 2005. The alternative marketplace will use the same infrastructure (the SAXESS trading system) as is used by OMX. The alternative marketplace will give smaller companies more visibility.

Harmonized cash market

As part of the process of creating an integrated Nordic and Baltic market, OMX has harmonized the cash markets thus providing additional customer benefits, such as harmonized trading hours, harmonized fee structures and harmonized trading rules between the Finnish and Swedish cash markets.

DMA to increase liquidity

The OMX Exchange has also launched direct market access (DMA) which allows accredited firms to nominate clients, such as fund managers, to enter orders directly into the system to be submitted to the market. DMA will be directly linked to the SAXESS platform. This increases the remote membership to the exchange and permits clients from the US or the Asia-Pacific region to trade on the exchange. The launching of DMA has great potential for increasing the liquidity of the NOREX Alliance.

The OMX Exchange has integrated the Nordic/Baltic region. The NOREX Alliance is the first stock exchange alliance in the world to implement a common system for share trading and to harmonize the trading and membership rules and regulations for exchanges in different countries. It is the best example of a modern-day stock exchange. It has been formed by the integration and consolidation of a few national stock exchanges which by themselves were too small. The OMX Exchange has integrated equity and derivatives exchanges and trades, on two separate trading platforms. Being a technology provider itself, the exchange has developed fully automatic systems for trading, clearing and settling functions.

The OMX Exchange has truly emerged as the exchange of the future. Being a technology provider for most stock exchanges of the world, they have the best technology in use, from the trading system to clearing and settlement systems. After harmonizing the fee structure, the exchange is charging a unified fee from any access point. Moreover, being a fully electronic trading system, the fees are much lower compared to other exchanges. Besides, by permitting DMA to access the NOREX Alliance, the exchange expects to increase liquidity too.

New York Stock Exchange

An ancient, well-developed, self-regulated exchange

The New York Stock Exchange (NYSE) has a 212-year history of securities trading in the USA. It is the world's largest cash equities market. At the end of December 2004, 2768 companies, totaling $20tn in global market capitalization, listed their shares on the NYSE. The exchange still operates as a member-owned, non-profit organization. Despite its long history, the exchange still operates from the trading floor. The NYSE uses a combination of individual specialists and brokers supported by technology to offer the best possible market prices.

The NYSE brings buyers and sellers together in one centralized agency auction market (the NYSE trading floor). It is one of the few exchanges still operating a traditional trading pit or floor.

The NYSE plays a critical role in the US securities industry as an SRO. The NYSE examines and enforces financial and operational rules and codes of conduct for members and member organizations. The NYSE is responsible for the regulatory oversight of its members' trading activities. The exchange is also responsible for ensuring that companies listed on it comply with the listing requirements of the exchange and other corporate governance requirements.

Evolution of the Exchange

Buttonwood Tree Agreement

The origins of the NYSE can be traced to the Buttonwood Tree Agreement of 1792. Twenty-four prominent brokers and merchants gathered on Wall Street to sign the Buttonwood Tree Agreement, agreeing to trade securities on a commission basis. The NYSE traces its beginnings to this historic pact.

In 1817, the New York brokers established a formal organization, the New York Stock & Exchange Board, and rented rooms at 40 Wall Street. They then adopted a constitution with rules for the conduct of business. These business rules set the initial governing rules which in a crude way regulated the markets.

Technological developments have been incorporated since time immemorial

Technological developments like the telegraph and cable services immensely benefited the communication network between brokers and investors outside New York as well as in London. The NYSE began to gain trading orders from outside New York as well as outside the country, thus increasing volumes. The exchange consequently tightened the listing norms in 1853. However, the trading volumes continued to rise and the exchange began to supervise and control listing policies.

In 1868, the membership right on the exchange became a property right, whereby "members" could buy and sell "seats" on the exchange.

In 1871, the exchange began continuous trading via specialists. To foster more liquid markets, the NYSE adopted a system of continuous trading, replacing calls of stocks at set times. As part of the new system, brokers dealing in a particular stock remained at one location on the trading floor, which gave rise to "specialists".

In 1878, the first telephone was installed on the NYSE floor, just two years after its invention by Alexander Graham Bell.

The first clearing house of the exchange

In 1892, NYSE established the New York Stock Exchange Clearing House to centralize and expedite the transfer of securities from broker to broker.

Seeds of regulations

In 1895, NYSE first recommended that all listed companies send their stockholders annual reports with an income statement and balance sheet. In 1899, this was made a mandatory requirement.

In 1903, the NYSE moved to new premises – its current location – on 18 Broad Street. The trading floor is still in use today. However, currently the trading floor is 60 percent larger than the original floor built in 1903.

CCP clearing established

In 1920, the NYSE established The Stock Clearing Corporation, a CCP clearing system, for developing a centralized system for delivering and clearing securities among members, banks and trust companies.

Listing rules

In 1926, the exchange tightened the listing rules to encourage companies to give equal voting rights to stockholders.

In 1929, the exchange installed the "central quote system" to provide instantaneous bid-ask prices by phone.

In 1939, the NYSE opened the trading floor gallery to the public. The gallery is known today as the Interactive Education Center.

In 1957, the Ebasco Services Report issued its report on the possibility of automating the trading floor. The report contained suggestions for automating transaction reporting, and improved stock clearing and quotation service.

In 1966, the NYSE created the composite index of all listed common stocks. This was referred to as the Common Stock Index and was transmitted daily. The starting point of the index was 50. It was later renamed the NYSE Composite Index.

Subsequently, from December 1966, the exchange began transmitting fully automated trade and quote data from the floor of the exchange.

DTC established

As trading volumes grew, member firms struggled to process transactions on time. The "paperwork crisis" continued for months, spurring increased automation. So, in 1968, the exchange established the Central Certificate Service to transfer securities electronically, eliminating their physical handling for settlement purposes. Later, in 1978, the exchange established the Depository Trust Company (DTC) to provide a central depository for securities certificates and electronically record transfers of stock ownership.

ITP for upgrading trading floor

In 1993, the NYSE commenced the Integrated Technology Plan (ITP) for upgrading the trading floor networks, hardware and software, thereby enhancing the quality, capacity, efficiency and productivity of virtually every aspect of trading floor operations. On completion, the systems capacity was enhanced to handle over one billion trades a day.

In 1995, the NYSE launched an aggressive plan to reengineer the NYSE trading floor to make use of the most sophisticated technology of the time. Handheld terminals, fiberoptics, cellular communications and the first large-scale application of high-definition, flat-screen technology were installed to speed market information and strengthen trading floor professionals' ability to manage orders. At the same time, the exchange also introduced the three-day settlement period for listed equities.

In 1996, the NYSE launched real-time stock tickers on CNBC and CNN-FN. Prior to that, the display of market data was delayed by 20 minutes.

In 1997, the NYSE launched the Wireless Data System which permitted brokers to receive orders, access market information and transmit execution reports from any location on the trading floor.

In 1999, the NYSE unveiled the 3D Trading Floor, an advanced trading floor operations center.

NYSE Direct+

In 2001, the exchange launched a new trading service – NYSE Direct+. This was an automatic execution service for limit orders up to 1099 shares. This was the NYSE's biggest move towards electronic trading.

In August 2004, the NYSE filed with the SEC its plans to expand its trading system – the NYSE Direct+. If approved by regulators, limits will be eliminated on the size, timing, and types of orders that can be submitted via Direct+, significantly increasing the level of purely electronic trading at the NYSE.

In April 2005, the NYSE and ArcaEx announced their plans to enter a definitive merger agreement leading to a combined entity, NYSE Group, Inc. This merged entity will become a publicly held company if approved by regulators and will emerge as the largest securities exchange in the world.

The NYSE has a long and chequered history and along its evolutionary path it has adopted many innovative systems to emerge as the awe-inspiring exchange that it is today.

Governance Reforms

During 2003, the NYSE became embroiled in a number of controversies including:

- Accusations that member (specialist) firms were trading ahead of their clients

- Concerns about the governance of the exchange, particularly the inclusion on the board of directors of senior figures from firms which are themselves regulated by the NYSE

- Complaints about the chairman's remunerations.

Subsequently, the NYSE implemented new governance reforms from December 2003. As per the reforms, for the first time in the history of the exchange, its board was to be independent from both the exchange's management and members and also listed companies. The board of the exchange would be elected and held responsible for good corporate governance. The board would consist of six to twelve individuals elected annually in June.

The board of directors would appoint a chairman and a CEO – unless it decides that one person is qualified to fill both roles. The board will have to meet every quarter. Besides supervising the NYSE's regulatory function, the board will also be responsible for monitoring marketplace performance and competitive position, approving strategy, hiring, firing and paying management, and ensuring appropriate behavior.

A chief regulatory officer will report to the newly created regulatory oversight committee which consists solely of independent directors. The committee will determine the exchange's regulatory plan, programs, budget and staffing proposals annually. Richard Ketchum was appointed as the first chief regulatory officer.

Further, the board of directors will be assisted by a 20-member board of executives. The board of executives will represent key NYSE constituents, such as listed companies, NYSE lessors, broker-dealers, institutional investors, large public funds and individual investors. The board of executives will meet at least six times a year and will advise the board of directors on NYSE operations, market structure and performance issues. It will also meet jointly with the board of directors, and its lessor and floor representatives will meet separately with the board of directors annually.

Three committees consisting exclusively of independent directors play key roles in the governance of the NYSE. These are the Human Resources and Compensation Committee, the Audit Committee and the Nominating and Governance Committee. While the Human Resources and Compensation Committee will fix the remuneration of the exchange staff, the Audit Committee will oversee the exchange's financials and ensure proper internal audits and the Nominating Committee will structure the board's annual self-evaluation and propose a slate of directors for election by the members every year.

Since the implementation of these reforms, the exchange has been successful in implementing enhanced governance, transparency and reporting standards required of its listed companies, including new governance reforms and the unprecedented disclosure of financial information.

Hybrid Market

Combination of auction market and auto-execution

In 2005, the NYSE plans to launch a new market for trading securities – the hybrid market. The hybrid market is a combination of the auction market and auto-execution. Once implemented, it will be the first of its kind for trading equities. Limits will be eliminated on the size, timing and types of orders that can currently be submitted via the NYSE Direct+ automatic execution service. New features will be incorporated, giving customers a greater ability to trade electronically, with speed, certainty and anonymity. Interaction of the electronic and floor markets in the hybrid model will maintain the opportunity for price improvement, ensuring that the NYSE continues to provide the lowest execution costs, with higher liquidity, but with the smallest spreads and best execution in its listed stocks.

The NYSE hybrid market will integrate into one platform the best aspects of both the auction market and automatic trading. It is an innovative response to customer needs, creating a market that is faster and more flexible. The hybrid market will also give NYSE customers a broader array of trading choices than any other market, expanding access to the world's deepest pool of equity liquidity.

Specialists will continue to be a catalyst for bringing buyers and sellers together in the auction, and will supplement liquidity to stabilize price movements in both the automatic and auction components of the hybrid market. Floor brokers will participate both electronically and in person, using judgment to represent large orders more effectively than a purely electronic platform.

New Technology

During 2004, the exchange developed new technologies for the enhancement of the trading systems. They are as follows:

■ Further enhancements to NYSE Direct+ were built to provide institutional traders with automatic execution service for short sales and other special order types, when enabled.

■ The delivery time for automated executions on NYSE Direct+ was reduced, to a 0.6 second turnaround time through all NYSE systems.

■ New e-broker wireless handheld technology was developed to lay the foundation for floor professionals' full electronic participation in the hybrid market. Advanced features include a new wireless network with 50 times more capacity and a new handheld device with software that provides the capability to layer the book with interest at multiple price points.

■ NYSE Open Book Real-Time was developed to provide a vital information tool in the hybrid market and was added to floor brokers' handheld devices.

■ New technology, introduced successfully in the ETF market, was built to allow NYSE specialists to react more quickly by electronically publishing quotations, an important component of the hybrid market.

- NYSE systems capacity expanded from 6000 to 8000 messages per second, in preparation for further growth in customer message traffic.

- Floor brokers adopted wireless handheld technology, with about 800 daily wireless users on the NYSE trading floor, eliminating the need to support paper interactions in the hybrid market.

- The NYSE's business continuity plan was enhanced, with all post-9/11 improvements in network resilience completed, including a remote staffed network operations center located outside New York City.

Regulatory Reforms

The regulatory reforms initiated by the exchange in 2004 have been quite successful. Besides imposing disciplinary fines on defaulting member firms or their representatives, the NYSE regulations are trying to develop a culture of compliance framework. This will ensure the integrity of the market. NYSE regulations have provided member firms with clear, rule-based guidance with regard to the compliance control environment. The regulatory bodies are working closely with each specialist firm to help to build an effective compliance framework. Training has been enhanced to ensure that the NYSE staff are abreast of industry best practice norms.

The NYSE regulations have adopted a more risk-based approach in all areas of regulation. The Member Firm Regulation Division expanded and refined its risk selection criteria for conducting examinations in order to more effectively target reviews of new areas.

The Market Surveillance Division has analyzed and strengthened numerous trading surveillances. A new

Risk Analysis Unit was also created to protect investors by anticipating and assessing new securities products, the sales practices of brokers and the business operations of member organizations that are in potential violation of exchange rules.

In February 2005, the NYSE launched eGovDirect. com, a website to assist its listed companies with the electronic submission and management of their corporate compliance information. eGovDirect is an interactive tool developed by the exchange to bring greater efficiency to the corporate governance reporting processes.

NYSE and Archipelago to Merge

In April 2005, the NYSE and the Archipelago Exchange (ArcaEx) announced plans to merge, if approved by the country's regulators. The merged entity will create the world's largest equity market, with the most successful totally open, fully electronic exchange, creating long-term stockholder value. It will also enhance the depth and resilience of the US capital market by bringing together the strength of the NYSE's auction market and the speed and entrepreneurialism of Archipelago.

Archipelago is the first totally open, all-electronic stock market in the USA. Through its alliance with Pacific Stock Exchange, it operates as the exclusive equities trading facility of PCX Equities, Inc. Through ArcaEx, customers can trade over 8000 equity securities, including securities listed on the NYSE.

Since the 1990s, the NYSE has been introducing technology into its trading processes. Although it has yet to set up a fully electronic trading system due to the resistance of its floor traders and specialists, it has introduced substantial electronic medium into the intermediating trading system.

Surprisingly, while a number of smaller exchanges have demutualized, the NYSE has not yet succumbed. In 1999, the exchange did make an attempt towards it but had to give up its plans due to resistance from specialists and floor brokers.

If the merger with Archipelago takes place, not only will the exchange update to a fully electronic trading system, it may also be demutualized sooner or later.

National Stock Exchange of India

Many firsts to its credit

The National Stock Exchange of India (NSE) was set up to play a leading role in enlarging the scope of market reforms in India. In the past decade, the NSE has been a catalyst in reforming the markets and developing market efficiencies with the investor in mind. The exchange was set up on a demutualized model, wherein the ownership, management and trading rights are in the hands of three different sets of people. This has completely eliminated conflicts of interest. This in turn has helped the NSE to aggressively pursue policies for the benefit of investors. NSE's nationwide, automated trading system has helped in shifting the trading platform from the trading hall at the exchange's premises to the computer terminals at the premises of the trading members located at different places in the country and subsequently to the PCs in investors' homes and even to the portable handheld devices of mobile investors.

The NSE has been encouraging the corporatization of membership in the securities market. It has been instrumental in ushering in scriptless trading in India and providing settlement guarantee for all trades executed on the exchange. Settlement risks have been eliminated by the establishment of the clearing corporation (NSCCL), the settlement guarantee fund (SGF), the reduction of settlement cycle, and by implementing online, real-time risk management systems, dematerialization and electronic transfer of securities. The market today uses state-of-the-art IT to provide an efficient and transparent trading, clearing and settlement mechanism. For protecting the investors who have incurred financial loss due to default of brokers, the NSE has created the investors protection fund (IPF).

Scaling heights quickly

The NSE has quickly gained popularity and has been ranked among the world top ten derivatives exchanges. It was ranked second in the world by the World Federation of Exchanges in the number of stock option contracts offered during 2004 and seventh in stock options trading volume during the same period. During 2004, it was also ranked second in the number of stock index futures contracts, while CME ranked fourth. Similarly, in the value of bond trading, NSE ranked tenth among its global peers in 2004.

Evolution of the Exchange

India has had a stock market since 1887, when the first stock exchange – the Bombay Stock Exchange – began trading. The Bombay Stock Exchange was considered the premier stock exchange in the country. But a decade ago, with the liberalization process in the background, financial irregularities came to the forefront. It was evident then that reform in the capital market was crucial. The creation of an independent capital market regulator initiated this reform process. The securities market regulator, the Securities and Exchange Board of India (SEBI), was established in 1988 and became a fully autonomous body by 1992, with defined responsibilities to cover the development and regulation of the capital markets. SEBI highlighted the inefficiencies of the bourses and recommended that the capital markets required better regulation, discipline and accountability. A committee recommended the creation of a second stock exchange in Mumbai called the National Stock Exchange. This committee also suggested the formation of an exchange which would link investors across the length and breadth of the country into a single, screen-based trading platform.

A technologically linked exchange

It was on this recommendation that a technologically linked exchange was conceptualized. The trading system of the NSE is a totally integrated and automated screen-based trading system. The NSE was incorporated in 1992 and was recognized as a stock exchange in 1993. It started operating in June 1994 with trading on the wholesale debt market segment. It launched the capital market segment in November 1994 for trading in equities and the futures and options segment in June 2000 for trading in derivative products.

Owned by FIs, banks and insurance companies

The NSE is owned by a few leading financial institutions, banks, insurance companies and other financial intermediaries. It is managed by a team of professional managers and the trading rights are with trading members who offer their services to the investors. The board of directors of the NSE comprises senior executives from promoter institutions and eminent professionals. There are no representatives of trading members on the board of directors.

Managed by an independent board

While the board deals with the broad policy issues, the executive committees (ECs), which include trading members, formed under the articles of association and the rules of the NSE for different market segments, set out the rules and parameters to manage the day-to-day affairs of the NSE. The executive committees have formed several committees, such as the Committee on Trade Related Issues and the Committee on Settlement Issues, comprising mostly trading members, to receive inputs from market participants and implement suggestions which are in the best interest of the investors and the market. The day-to-day management of the exchange is delegated to the managing director and CEO who are supported by a team of professional staff. Therefore, although the role of trading members at the NSE is only that of providing trading services to investors, the NSE involves trading members in the process of consultation and participation in vital inputs towards decision making.

Market Segments and Products

A well-integrated exchange providing trading facilities for all types of securities

The NSE provides an electronic trading platform for all types of securities for investors under one roof – equities, corporate debts, government bonds, Treasury bills, commercial papers (CPs), certificate of deposits (CDs), warrants, mutual fund units, ETFs and derivatives products. The NSE is one of the few exchanges in the world providing trading facilities for all types of securities on a single exchange. The exchange provides trading in three different segments – the wholesale debt market (WDM), the capital market (CM) and the futures and options (F&O) market.

The **Wholesale Debt Market** – Provides the trading platform for trading a wide range of debt securities which includes state and central government securities, T-bills, PSU bonds, corporate debentures, CPs, CDs, and so on. Along with these standard instruments, the NSE has also launched certain innovative products.

MIBID/MIBOR

Interest rates play a vital role in the banking sector and are closely monitored by market participants. The NSE started computing and disseminating the NSE Mumbai Inter-bank Bid Rate (MIBID) and NSE

Mumbai Inter-bank Offer Rate (MIBOR). Since a reference rate is an accurate measure of the market price, most money market participants monitor the NSE MIBID/MIBOR rates closely.

Zero coupon yield curve

Banks, financial institutions, mutual funds and insurance companies have substantial investments in sovereign securities. To meet the lacuna in this sector, the NSE started dissemination of another product – the zero coupon yield curve. This product helps in the valuation of sovereign securities across all maturities, irrespective of its liquidity in the market.

NSE Government Securities Index

India has witnessed increased trading activity in the government securities market. Mutual fund products have also emerged as the most preferred investment option. This gave rise to the need for a well-defined bond index to measure returns in the bond market. The NSE filled this lacuna by constructing the NSE Government Securities Index. This index provides a benchmark for portfolio management by various investment managers and gilt funds.

Trading system

The WDM trading system is known as the National Exchange for Automated Trading – NEAT. The WDM trading system provides two market sub-types: the continuous market and the negotiated market. In the continuous market, the buyer and the seller do not know each other and they put their best buy/sell orders, which are stored in the order book with price/time priority. If orders match, it results in trade. The trades in the WDM segment are settled directly between the participants.

In the negotiated market, the trades are normally decided by the seller and the buyer outside the exchange, and reported to the exchange through a trading member for approval.

NEAT trading system

The **Capital Market** segment – Also offers a screen-based trading system – the NEAT system. The NEAT system is quite efficient and enables members from across the country to trade with enormous ease and efficiency on a price/time priority basis. Various types of securities – equity shares, warrants, debentures, and so on – are traded on the NEAT.

The **Futures and Options** segment – Offers trading in derivatives instruments like index futures, index options, stock options, stock futures and futures on interest rates. Although it has only been introduced for four years, it has been well accepted and made a mark for itself globally.

Trading system

The derivatives trading system at the NSE is called the NEAT F&O trading system. It is a fully automated screen-based trading system for all types of derivatives products. It supports an anonymous order-driven market, which operates on a strict price/time priority. It provides tremendous flexibility to users in terms of the kinds of orders that can be placed into the system.

Technology

Significant reliance on technology

The NSE was formed as the most technologically developed exchange in South Asia. The aim of the exchange was to provide the investing community and market participants with the best technology, while keeping costs as low as possible. The NSE chose to harness technology in creating a new market design. Since technology provides the necessary impetus for a fully developed capital market, the NSE has developed a fully integrated trading system. Technology enables an organization to retain its competitive edge and ensure timeliness and satisfaction to customers.

First exchange to use satellite communication technology in trading

The NSE has stressed innovation and sustained investment in technology to remain ahead of competition. The NSE is the first exchange in the world to use satellite communication for trading. It uses satellite communication technology to energize participation through about 2829 very small aperture terminals from 345 cities across the country.

The exchange's trading system – NEAT – is a state-of-the-art client server-based application. At the server end all trading information is stored in an in-memory database to achieve minimum response time and maximum system availability for users. The NSE has continuously undertaken capacity enhancement measures so as to effectively meet the requirements of the increase in users and the associated trading loads. Recently, the NSE has further enhanced its capacity to handle up to six million trades per day. The NSE has also put in place its internet-based information system – NIBIS – for online, real-time dissemination of trading information over the internet.

Disaster backup hub with identical facilities and real time back-up

As part of its business continuity plan, the NSE has established a disaster backup site at Chennai along with its entire infrastructure, including the satellite earth station and the high-speed fiberoptic link with its main office at Mumbai. The Chennai backup hub is a replica of the environment at Mumbai. The transactions are backed up on a real-time basis from the main site to the disaster backup site to keep both sites synchronized at all times with each other.

The exchange has a 100 percent subsidiary NSE.IT Ltd to provide thrust to NSE's technology edge, concomitant with its overall goal of harnessing the latest technology for optimum business use. It provides the securities industry with technology that ensures transparency and efficiency in trading, clear-

ing and risk management systems. NSE.IT also
provides consultancy services in the areas of data
warehousing, internet and business continuity plans.

Clearing and Settlement

NSCCL set up in 1995

NSE set up its subsidiary National Securities Clearing
Corporation Ltd (NSCCL) in August 1995 and began
clearing activities in April 1996. It was the first clearing
corporation in the country to provide novation/settle-
ment guarantee that revolutionalized the entire concept
of settlement in India. It was set up to promote and
maintain short and consistent settlement cycles,
provide counterparty risk guarantee, and operate a tight
risk containment system. NSCCL carries out the clearing and settlement of trades (both equity as well as
derivatives) executed on the NSE. It operates a well-
defined settlement cycle and there are no deviations or
deferments from this cycle. It aggregates trades over a
trading period T, nets the positions to determine the
liabilities of members and ensures movement of funds
and securities to meet respective liabilities.

The NSCCL also operates a subsidiary general ledger
(SGL) for settling trades in government securities for
its constituents. It has been managing clearing and
settlement functions since its inception, without a
single failure.

The NSCCL has tied up with ten clearing banks for
funds settlement while it has direct connectivity with
depositories for settlement of securities. It has also initiated a working capital facility in association with the
clearing members to meet their working capital requirements. The NSCCL has also introduced the facility of
direct payout to clients' accounts on the depositories.

The NSCCL currently settles trades under a T+2 rolling settlement. It continuously upgrades the clearing and settlement procedures and has also brought Indian financial markets in line with international markets.

Settlement Guarantee Fund

The NSCCL has set up the Settlement Guarantee Fund (SGF) through the contributions of its trading members. The SGF is intended primarily to guarantee completion of settlement up to the normal payout for trades executed in the regular market and will not act as guarantee for company objection cases.

The SGF therefore ensures that the settlement is not held up on account of the failure of trading members to meet their obligations and all market participants (trading members, custodians, investors and so on) who have completed their part of the obligations are not affected in any way whatsoever.

Depository Services

NSDL

Prior to the dematerialization of shares, they had to be physically transferred from the seller to the buyer through a long chain of intermediaries (seller to seller's broker-trader, seller's broker-trader to buyer's broker-trader, and buyer's broker-trader to buyer). This involved a long time lag and the risk of delay or loss in the chain of events. Further, the system of transfer of ownership was grossly inefficient as every transfer required paper work. In many cases the transfer time required was much greater than that stipulated.

All this added to the costs and delays in settlement and consequently curtailed liquidity in the market. To eradicate these problems and promote dematerialization, the NSE set up the National Securities Depository Limited (NSDL) in collaboration with the Unit Trust of India and Industrial Development Bank of India. The depository system gained quick acceptance and was able to achieve the objective of eradicating paper from the trading and settlement of securities.

Investor Grievances

Investor protection forms the crux of any exchange and the NSE is no different. The NSE has put in place systems to ensure the availability of adequate, up-to-date and correct information to investors to enable them to take informed decisions. It ensures that critical and price-sensitive information reaching the exchange is made available to all investors at the same point of time. The exchange can initiate action against listed companies if they fail to provide information within a stipulated time to their investors through the exchange. In an attempt to ease the existing system of information dissemination by listed companies, the NSE launched an electronic interface for listed companies in August 2004. Under the new system, all corporate announcements, including that of board meetings, which need to be disclosed to the market are handled electronically in a straight through and hands-free manner.

Investor Grievance Cell

The NSE has set up the Investor Grievance Cell (IGC), which is manned by professionals who possess the relevant experience in the areas of securities markets, company and legal affairs and are specially trained to identify problems faced by investors and find a solution quickly. It takes up complaints in respect of trades executed on the NSE through its NEAT terminal and routed through the NSE trading member or the SEBI-registered sub-broker of the NSE trading member and trades pertaining to companies traded on NSE.

Investor Protection Fund The NSE also set up the Investor Protection Fund to take care of investor claims, which may arise out of the non-settlement of obligations by a trading member, who may have been declared a defaulter, in respect of trades executed on the NSE.

SFE Corporation Ltd

The SFE Corporation Ltd (SFE), formerly known as the Sydney Futures Exchange, was established in 1960 to provide hedging facilities for merino wool. It was then known as the Sydney Greasy Wool Futures Exchange.

The SFE is currently one of the major derivatives exchanges in the world. Its four major products – the 3-year Australian Treasury Bond Futures, the 10-Year Australian Treasury Bond Futures, the 90-Day Australian Bank Accepted Bill Futures and the SFE SPI 200 Equity Index Futures – are all ranked among the top traded futures products in the Asia-Pacific region. Apart from interest rate and equity index futures, the SFE also offers options on futures, equity options, individual share futures, currency futures and commodity futures on its fully electronic 24-hour trading system.

Evolution of the Exchange

A demutualized exchange listed on the ASX

Formed in 1960, the Sydney Futures Exchange was demutualized after four decades in September 2000. In January 2002, the SFE Group was restructured and the SFE Corporation became the holding company of the four subsidiaries. In April 2002, SFE Corporation shares were listed on the ASX.

The SFE establishes a clearing house

In 1991, the SFE established its own clearing house – the SFE Clearing Corporation Pty Ltd. In December

2000, it merged the clearing house with the major Australian clearing house – Austraclear. The combined entity is known as SFE Clearing.

All trades executed at SFE Corporation are cleared through SFE Clearing which provides novation services, interposing itself between the buyer and the seller and acting as the central counterparty to all trades. It is backed by an A$177m guarantee to guard against defaults by clearing participants.

The SFE developed the world's first after-hour's electronic trading platform – SYSCOM – in 1989. Prior to that the exchange used the open outcry method of trading from the traditional trading floor. In 1999, the exchange closed the trading floor and moved all its trading to the electronic platform. This was accompanied by an expansion of SFE's proprietary communications network, with hubs installed in the USA and Europe, as well as throughout the Asia-Pacific region. To facilitate connectivity to its network, SFE introduced a trading interface allowing customers to utilize their regular trading front end in addition to SFE's SYSCOM terminals. SYSCOM offers a 24-hour trading facility to SFE's clients.

In December 2001, SFE introduced the OM SECUR clearing and settlement platform to all clearing participants. OM SECUR (developed by the Swedish group OM) is used by a number of exchanges around the world as their derivatives clearing platform. Subsequently, in 2002, SFE entered into an agreement with OM to outsource its clearing system development and maintenance activities. Under the agreement, OM and SFE will jointly develop an over-the-counter securities clearing and settlement system to be named EXIGO CSD. This new clearing and settlement system will replace the existing FINTRACS system of Austraclear.

EXIGO CSD is expected to be complete by the second half of 2005. On completion of this new platform, the SFE will have one common infrastructure for the clearing and settlement of derivatives contracts as well as for over-the-counter debt securities. The SFE will also extend its Austraclear franchise into multicurrency CSD services, in keeping with the trend towards greater issuance and holdings of non-Australian-dollar-based securities by Australian banks and non-financial corporations. It will also widen its franchise into other asset classes and business-to-business clearing and settlement applications. OM has already taken over the operations and maintenance of both OM SECUR and FINTRACS, and will do the same for EXIGO CSD once it is installed.

Emphasis on Technological Developments

Automated 24-hour
trading

A major cornerstone of SFE's business strategy has been its focus on technological developments. The exchange has been providing its clients with a 24-hour electronic trading capability on its SYCOM trading system. The SFE has also set up communication hubs in the major financial centers around the world (including Auckland, Wellington, Hong Kong, Tokyo, London, Melbourne and Chicago), allowing customers in those centers direct access to the SYCOM trading platforms. SFE's trading interface also allows customers to use their trading front end of choice in addition to the SYCOM terminals.

Central to the success of the overseas hubs and trading volume to SFE is the process of enhancing accessibility to SYCOM. In May 2001, SFE's business rules were amended significantly to allow the clients of full participants direct connection to the SYCOM trading system. This enables full participants to provide improved access and functionality to their clients located near an SFE communications hub and provides speed of execution that is essential for large volume trading customers. Moreover, by providing non-participant users with the technology, SFE becomes a more attractive trading location.

The commissioning of EXIGO, expected by the second half of 2005, will provide the SFE with one common infrastructure for the clearing and settlement of derivative contracts as well as for over-the-counter debt securities.

Strategic Overseas Partnerships

The SFE has been exploring the possibility of cooperation with overseas exchanges in the Asia-Pacific region, with the general objective of deriving mutual benefits with respect to new product development, the creation of cross-border clearing opportunities or sharing technology infrastructure. In 2001, it signed an MoU with Hong Kong Exchanges, Osaka Securities Exchange and Tokyo International Financial Futures Exchange for this purpose. However, significant material benefits are yet to accrue from these. The SFE signed an MoU with the Shanghai Futures Exchange in September 2004 and another with the CBOT in October 2004.

SFE begins trading of New Zealand derivative products

The SFE and the New Zealand Exchange (NZX) have signed a deal whereby New Zealand equity derivative products will be listed and traded on the SFE. Subsequently NZFOE, a subsidiary of SFE, has ceased to operate and existing NZFOE products have been listed on the SFE. The deal is worth approximately A$1m for

SFE, while it gives NZX the exclusive ability to list a broad range of futures and options products on the SFE for a period of up to eight years. NZX will take full responsibility for branding the new futures and options products, and for the marketing and promotion of those products under the name NZFOX. The products will clear and settle through SFE Clearing Corporation.

The SFE has a proprietary communications network with hubs in Auckland, Wellington, Hong Kong, Tokyo, London, Melbourne and Chicago, allowing customers in those centers direct access to the SYCOM trading platforms. The hub volumes grew substantially in the first half of 2003 due to the distribution efforts put in during 2002 and the interest differentials and volatility in the US markets during the overnight trading sessions.

Development of New Products

The SFE regularly introduces innovative products

SFE has been quite innovative in launching new products and creating a market among its investor clients. It introduced two off-market trading facilities – block trade facility and exchange of futures for physical. It also launched a range of international bond spread futures and made it possible to trade cross-border bond spreads at one price in one market at one time. This product can be traded through all SFE hubs, including Sydney, Chicago, London, Hong Kong and Wellington.

SFE also launched the SFE SPI 200 Intra-Day Options (SPIDO), which is the first equity intra-day option from the basket of Interest Rate One-session Options product at SFE. This innovative product is a cash settled equity option contract with a life span of just one day.

In April 2005, the SFE and the Australian Financial Markets Association (AFMA) launched a new futures contract based on the AFMA Fixed Interest (FIX). The SFE has been developing debt derivatives for many years and this new contract is a logical complement to the highly successful 3- and 10-year Treasury Bond contracts.

The exchange also launched the SFE Listed Property Trust Futures contract in June 2005.

Being the innovative exchange that SFE is, it will continue to introduce innovative products on the exchange in the future.

REFERENCES

Allen, F. and Santomero, A.M. (1999) What do financial intermediaries do?, *Journal of Banking and Finance*, **25**, pp. 271–94.

Best, Katrina, *Global Stock Exchanges*, www.times-publications.com.

Buckner, John, *The Future of Securities Industries*, www.symphoni.com/pages/news/whitePapers/.

Clearing and Settlement in the European Union – The Way Forward, Commission of the European Communities (April 2004).

ECB (European Central Bank) *Blue Book of Payment and Securities Settlement in the European Union* (European Central Bank, Issues 2001–2003).

Foley and Lardner (2005) *SOX Impact on Private Companies*, White Paper.

Giddy, I., Saunders, A. and Walter, I. (1996) Alternative Models for Clearance and Settlement: the Case of the Single European Capital Market, *Journal of Money, Credit and Banking*, **28**(4) November.

Giovannini Group, The (2001, 2003) *Cross-border Clearing and Settlement Arrangements in the European Union*.

Kolman, Joe (2002) *Aftershocks: European Exchanges Focus on Post-Merger Integration*, www.WallStreetContent.com.

Lee, Ruben (2000) *What is an Exchange? The Automation, Management and Regulation of Financial Markets*, Oxford University Press.

Lee, Ruben (2002) *Capital Markets that Benefit Investors: A Survey of the Evidence on Fragmentation, Internalization and Market Transparency*, Oxford Finance Group (September).

Lee, Ruben (2002) The Future of Securities Exchanges, paper prepared for the Brookings-Wharton Conference, January–February 2002. *Brookings-Wharton Papers on Financial Services*. Brookings Institution Press.

Litan, R.E. and Herring, R. (2001) The Future of Securities Markets, *Brookings-Wharton Papers on Financial Services 2002*.

McAndrews, James and Stefanadis, Chris (2002) The Consolidation of European Stock Exchanges, *Current Issues in Economics and Finance*, **8**(6) June.

Schmiedel, Heiko, Malkamäki, Markku and Tarkka, Juha, European Commission, Brussels, *Economies of Scale and Technological Development in Securities Depository and Settlement Systems*, (European Central Bank).

Skeete, Herbie (2003) *World Exchanges: Global Industry Outlook and Investment Analysis,* June, Mondo Visione.

Skeete, Herbie (ed.) (2005) *The Handbook of World Stock, Derivative and Commodity Exchanges,* www.researchandmarkets.com.

Smith, Karen M. (2000) The Need for Centralised Securities Regulation in the European Union. Boston College, *International and Comparative Law Review,* **24**(1).

Steil, Benn, Victor, David and Nelson, Richard (2002) *Technological Innovation and Economic Performance,* Princeton University Press.

Websites

Centre for European Policy Studies, www.ceps.be

Federation of European Securities Exchanges, www.fese.be

Financial Services Authority, www.fsa.gov.uk

Futures Industry Association, www.futuresindustry.org

Securities Industry Association, www.sia.com

US Securities and Exchange Commission, www.sec.gov

World Federation of Exchanges, www.world-exchanges.org